You

CHAMPAGNE ARDENNE

© May 2005 by Passport Guide Publications

Written &
  Compiled By: Sharron Livingston

Published By: Passport Guide Publications
Enquiries :   Tel: 020 8905 4851
Email: Sharron@channelhoppers.net
Web site: www.channelhoppers.net

All rights reserved.
No part of this publication may be reproduced, stored in a retrieval system or transmitted in any form or by any means, electronic, mechanical, photocopying, recording, or otherwise used in any form of advertising, sales promotion or publicity without the prior permission of Passport Guide Publications.

Notice:
Every effort has been made to ensure that this book contains accurate and current information at the time of going to print. We cannot be liable for any subsequent changes.

ISBN: 1903390052   First Edition

Contents

Topic	Page
Introduction	7
Map of Champagne-Ardenne	8
Hopping Over	9
Getting There	10
Where the Motorways Take You	11
Background	13
Ardennes	18
Map of Ardennes	19
Ardennes Must Sees	22
Legends along the Meuse	24
Givet	27
Charleville-Mézières	28
Charleville-Mézières Sights	31
Map of Charleville-Mézières	34
Marne	36
Map of Marne	37
Forêt d'Argonne	38
Epernay	39
Epernay Sights	40
Map of Epernay	42
Reims	43
Reims Sights	46
Map of Reims	48
Châlons-en-Champagne & Beyond	52
Sainte-Menehould	55

Contents

Topic	Page
Aube	56
Map of Aube	57
Aube Muse Sees	59
Les Riceys	60
Where to Buy Les Riceys Rosé wine	61
Forêt d'Orient & The Great Lakes	62
Troyes	65
Troyes - Factory & Shopping Outlets	69
Troyes - Speciality Shops	70
Map of Troyes	72
Troyes Sights	74
Essoyes - Renoir's Garden	75
Map of Essoyes	77
Chaource - The Town	78
Chaource - Sights	70
Haute Marne	80
Map of Haute Marne	81
Haute Marne Must Sees	82
Saint Dizier	83
Chaumont	84
Map of Chaumont	85
Chaumont Sights	86
Langres	87
Langres Sights	89
Map of Langres	92

Contents

Topic	Page
Champagne Wine - The History	94
Champagne Wine - The Making	96
Champagne Styles	99
Champagne Labels	101
Champagne Wine Routes	102
Champagne More than a Quaff?	108
Champagne Houses *	109
* see featured Champagnes opposite	

Gastronomy	132
Menu Guide	134
Cheese	140
Menu Reader	142
- Meat	142
- Fish	142
- Poultry, eggs & sauces	143
- Fruite & Vegetables and Miscellaneious items	144
- Sweet Tooth? & Coffee Styles	146
Restaurants	
- Ardennes, Charleville-Mézières	147
- Ardennes, Givet	147
- Ardennes Rethel	148
- Ardennes, Sedan	148
- Marnes, Reims	149
- Marnes, Epernay	152
- Marnes, Châlons-en-Champagne	154
- Marne, L'Epine	156
- Aube, Troyes	157
- Haut Marne, Chaumont	159
- Haut Marne, Colombey-les-Deux Eglises	159
- Haut Marne, Langres	160

Contents

There are over 2700 Champagne Houses in Champange. We have included a handful.

Champagne Houses Featured

-	Bartnicki Père et Fils	Aube	110
-	Beaumont de Crayères	Marne	110
-	Bollinger	Marne	111
-	Canard Duchêne	Marne	111
-	De Castellane	Marne	112
-	Château de Bligny	Aube	113
-	Drappier	Aube	114
-	François Brossolette	Aube	115
-	G de Bafontarc	Aube	115
-	Henri Giraud	Marne	116
-	Jack Therrey	Aube	117
-	Jean Velut	Aube	117
-	Lanson	Marne	117
-	Launois Père et Fils	Marne	118
-	Marcel Vérzien	Aube	119
-	Mercier	Marne	120
-	Michel Furdyna	Aube	121
-	Michel Leroy-Galland	Aube	121
-	Moët et Chandon	Marne	121
-	Moutard-Diligent	Aube	122
-	Mumm	Marne	123
-	Perrier Brigandat	Aube	123
-	Perrier Jouet	Marne	124
-	Pierre Garbais	Aube	125
-	Piper-Heidsieck	Marne	125
-	Pommery	Marne	126
-	Remy Massin & Fils	Aube	127
-	Ruinart	Marne	128
-	Taittinger	Marne	128
-	Veuve Cliquot Ponsardin	Marne	130
-	Vranken	Marne	131

Contents

Topic	Page
Hotels	161
- Ardennes, Charleville-Mézières	161
- Ardennes, Givet	161
- Ardennes, Sedan	161
- Ardennes, Signy-L'Abbaye	162
- Ardennes, Vouziers	162
- Marne, Châlons-en-Champagne	162
- Marne, Epernay	163
- Marne, Dizy-Epernay	164
- Marne, L'Epine	164
- Marne, Etoges	164
- Marne, Fér en Tardenoise	165
- Marne, Reims	165
- Marne, Sezanne	167
- Marne, Vertus	167
- Aube, Bar Sur Aube	168
- Aube, Essoyes	168
- Aube, Troyes	168
- Haut Marne, Chaumont	170
- Haut Marne, Langres	170
Festivals	171
Practical Pages	
Driving in France	173
En route essentials	173
Motorway and Roads	174
Filling up	175
Emergency Phrases	176
Money Matters	178
Out and About in France	180
Conversion Tables	183
Custom Guidelines	184
Currency Converter	185

Introduction

Champagne more than just a bottle of bubbles!

Just a two to three hour drive from coastal Northern France takes you to the the area of France beloved by the world for its romantic château notions and fabulous bubbly wine.

Even without its bubblicious nectar, the Champagne-Ardenne area has an abundance of touristic appeal. Some of its sights have managed to get themselves on the UNESCO World Heritage list and many of its fortified towns are still surrounded by old ramparts, and the glorious châteaux, half-timbered houses and churches are not just prolific but sometimes simply stunning.

The region is also endowed with some fabulous lakes that offer water sports for the active, as well as regional nature parks of the Montagne de Reims and the Forêt d'Orient for rambling and camping.

Champagne can be split into four defined areas: the rugged beauty of the Ardennes spilling over into Belgium; the Marne, its heart and soul, is made up of Epernay and Reims, areas not only full of gently rolling vine-covered hills and valleys but also home to major and some lesser known champagne houses; Aube, a region of great lakes, woodlands and whose famous town Troyes backs onto Burgundy; and towards the east is the Haute-Marne region full of lush and fertile lands.

It's not surprising that the major touristic appeal focuses on the area's most abundant produce - champagne, the Champagne houses that produce it and by extension the areas in which they are produced.

Festivals have developed around the grape harvest and the local saint, Saint Vincent is the patron saint of wine-growers. Each July a different village is bestowed with the honour of hosting a 'Tourist Champagne Route Festibulle' - a two day street festival of street theatre and dance with stands selling food and drink. It seems like good reason to celebrate Champagne. But then, any reason is a good reason to celebrate with bubbles.

Hopping Over

From	To	Company	Crossing Time	Frequency
Folkestone	**Calais Coquelles**	**Eurotunnel** Tel: 08705 353 535 No foot passengers Check in: 30 mins	35 mins	Every 15 minutes
Dover	**Calais Port**	**Hoverspeed** Tel: 0870 5240 241 Check in: 30 mins	60 mins	Hourly
		P&O Ferries Tel: 08705 202 020 Check in: 30 mins	75 mins	Every 45 mins at peak time
		SeaFrance Tel: 08705 711 711 Check in: 45 mins	90 mins	Every 90 mins at peak time
Dover	**Dunkirk**	**Norfolk Line** Tel: 0870 870 1020 Check in: 60 mins	120 mins	Every 4 hours
Dover	**Boulogne**	**Speedferries** www.speedferries.com	45 mins	5 a day

Getting There

Travelling to and from the major towns in Champagne -Ardenne is easy with numerous sign-posted routes taking drivers throughout the region. From Reims, the A26 can be taken to Troys and the N51 reaches to Givet. The following directions will get you to Reims.

From Calais to Reims:
Take A16/E402 motorway from Calais towards Dunkerque, Béthune and Lens. At Junction 47 head onto the A26/E15 towards St Omer, Arras, Reims, Paris. You have to pass through a toll booth. Leave the A26 at junction 16 signposted ZI Colbert, Reims-Champagne Driving time: 2.20 hrs

From Boulogne to Reims:
From the ferry terminal follow the signs to Le Touquet, Abbeville and the roundabout take 3rd exit onto N42. At next roundabout take 1st exit onto the N42. Stay on N42 over three roundbouts and on 3rd roundabout take 3rd exit to join A26 motorway. Leave the A26 at junction 16 signpoted ZI Colbert, Reims-Champagne: Driving time 2.30 hrs

From Dunkerque to Reims:
Head for D916 and turn left onto the A25 signposted A25 Steenvoorde, Lille. Continue onto A1 signposted A1 Valenciennes, A1 Gent (Gand), Bruxelles and join the A26 signposted A26 Cambrai, E17 Reims, Metz. Leave the A26 at junction 16 signpoted ZI Colbert, Reims-Champagne: Driving time 2.20 hrs

DRIVING TIMES AND TOLL CHARGES

From Calais to:	Driving Time Hours.Mins	Levy in Euros
Reims	2.20	16.30
Epernay	2.50	16.30
Châlons-en-Champagne	2.45	18.40
Charleville-Mézières	3.30	16.30
Sedan	3.30	15.70
Troyes	3.30	23.80
Bar-sur-Aube	4.15	28.20
Chaumont	4.15	29.40
Langres	4.30	31.40

NOTE.
As toll charges are subject to change without notice. Please use this table as a guide only. Driving times are approximate.

Where The Motorways Take You

Champagne-Ardennes is endowed with a great motorway system.
Here's an overview of where it takes you.

A4 Dorman Reims

Epernay, Neuvillette, Tinqueux, Cathédrale St Remi, Cormontreuil
These make up the Route Touristique du Champagne and lead through the Montagne de Reims or either the Marne Valley or Côte des Blancs. Reims is on the UNESCO's world heritage list and Epernay is the capital of the champagne area.

A4 Châlons-en-Champagne

La Veuve, St-Etienne au Temple St-Gibrien, Mont Choisy
Châlons-en-champagne is the regional capital. This exit leads to the small village of l'Epine (If passing remember to check out the Notre Dame Basilica - see page 54).

A4 Ste-Ménehould

This leads to the Argonne Massif where memories of the Great War still linger. Ste-Ménehould is the home of the famous Dom Pérignon and also famous for its pig trotters.

A26 - Charmont
A5 - St-Thibault

A26 Thénelières, A5 Thorvilliers
Exit here for the capital of Champagne: Troyes. Great for its churches, museums and factory shops. Go south west and you are in the cider country of Pays d'Othe.

Where The Motorways Take You

**A5
Magnant
Ville-sous-la Ferté**

Leads to Forêt d'Orient Regional Nature Reserve and also to Nigloland amusement park.

**A26
Vallée de l'aisne**

Follow this exit for the woodlands and the forests of the Ardennes.

**A26
Sommesous
Vallée de l'Aube**

This leads to over 10,0000 hectares of wonderful countryside between Troyes and St-Dizier as well as the lakes.

**A31
Langres Nord
Langres Sud**

Rolampont, Aubrive
Langres Nord located on a hill is a walled city with fantastic ramparts. Langres Sud is full of woodlands complete with deer.

**A31
Montigny-le Roi**

This region of the Haute Marne is famous for its cutlery making.

Background

**The Benedictine monks built the Abbey of Hautvillers in the 7th century.
Dom Pierre Perignon appeared in 1668.
The rest, as they say, is history!**

Medieval Times

In medieval times, the Champagne area was a mere duchy ruled for almost four hundred years (5th to 8th centuries) by Merovingian rulers - a race who were the descendants of the founder of the German Frankish dynasty, Merovech.

It got its name from the Latin word 'Campus' or 'campania' which simply means 'land of the plains'. In old French this became Champaign and finally evolved into its modern day version of 'Champagne'.

Amazingly, even before this time and certainly centuries before bubbles in wine became part of the vinous landscape, the actual art of viticulture had been documented in the Marne region of Champagne as long ago as 79 AD. Even more amazing is that fossil evidence shows wild vines were growing naturally in Marne and Epernay over a million years ago!

As early as 92 AD the wines of Champagne were recognised as great wines and this jolted the envious Emperor Domitian to decree that France's vineyards should be destroyed because they were proving to be too much competition for the wines produced in the Italian peninsula.

Rather than die away though, wine making in Champagne went underground and vineyards were cultivated in

> **Regional Tourist Board Champagne-Ardenne**
> 15 avenue du Maréchal leclerc
> Chalons-en-champagne
> Tel: 00 33 (0)326 21 85 80
> www.tourisme-champagne-ardenne.com
> contact@tourisme-champagne-ardenne.com

Background

secret. Fortunately, Emperor Probus rescinded the decree and the lost vineyards were eventually replaced.

The Romans created gigantic underground caverns, known as 'crayeres', in the chalk around Reims and Epernay and these are still used today as champagne cellars.

Incidentally, the White cliffs of Dover are formed by the same chalk subsoil which surfaces at Calais and forms the Mountain of Reims.

Monastic Influence

Religion has always featured as a powerful influence in all aspects of French life and this includes wine production. In fact, Christianity, to a great extent, was a blessing to Champagne and its wine production. This is because many vineyards had been, often inadvertently, bequeathed to the monastic orders. It was quite normal that while away on crusade, crusaders would entrust their property to the church for safe keeping and as many did not return, the monastic holdings were very much increased.

As a result, by the eleventh century, the wines produced by Champagne's coveted vineyards

Touring around Champagne you will see small buildings like these. They are called 'cadoles' and were once used by grape pickers to shelter from the rains.

Background

were the only ones considered worthy of being used as sacramental wine in front of God or King and in effect were nationalised in clerical hands.

Easy to Invade

Champagne's central location made it easy to invade and the region was a battlefield in 451 when Acius defeated Attila's Huns. During the Hundred Years' War and the Thirty Years' War the region was repeatedly destroyed as armies marched back and forth over the landscape. By the 17th century, Reims saw destruction seven times and Epernay at least twenty-five times.

World War I literally scorched Champagne's earth; many vineyards became battlefields and many cellars were emptied.

Once again in World War II the vineyards were battlefields and occupied by Nazis. Nevertheless, since the end of the last war, Champagne has managed to rebuild itself spectacularly well.

Commercial Prosperity

Yet the same geographic position that made Champagne vulnerable to invasion also endowed the region with an invasion of a commercial variety. Merchants from all over western Europe met at various markets six times each year, a tradition heartily encouraged by the Counts of Champagne. Their laws regulating trade had a profound influence on later commercial customs; for instance, the troy weight for precious metals is still used today.

As the next three hundred years passed the country became famous for its commercial fairs. These were held in Champagne's capital Troyes, Provins, Lagny-sur-Marne, and Bar-sur-Aube amidst a great deal of pomp.

> Did you know...
> that Champagne-Ardenne produces 25% of all the ice cream in France?

Background

Provins became the most prosperous town in France just behind Paris and Rouen and Bar-sur-Aube was the first town to be elevated by the Comtes de Champagne into a lucrative fair town.

The fairs reached their peak in the 12th century under Henri de Champagne who ensured the fairs were run justly by appointing legal specialists to preside over disputes.

With prosperity came cultural and architectural brilliance, illustrated superbly in the work of Chrétien de Troyes and in the Gothic cathedral at Reims.

By the 10th century the duchy had matured into a hereditary estate known as the county of Champagne and passed into the hands of the counts of Blois in the 11th century.

Joining the Royal Domain

Most famous of the counts was Thibaut IV a troubadour and a distinguished poet, who in 1234 inherited the crown of Navarre from his grandfather Sancho VII.

> **Q:** What is the difference between **le champagne** and **la Champagne.**
> **A:** Le champagne refers to the wine, la Champagne refers to the Champagne region of France where le champagne is produced.

He was succeeded by his elder son Theobald V of Champagne and then by his younger son Henry III of Champagne.

In 1286 the daughter and heir of the Count of Champagne (and King of Varre) Henry III, married Philip IV of France.

In 1314 Champagne's status changed when their son, Louis, succeeded as Louis X King of France, and the region became a province of the royal domain in France. He died suddenly just two years later but spent much of this time trying to raise money through stealth

> Did you know..
> The Champagne-Ardenne region encompasses 700,000 hectares of forests, a quarter of the region's surface.

Background

measures. The bishoprics of Reims and Langres were added later. After this, Champagne's prosperity began to decline but the enduring popularity of its bubbly wine brought a lasting sparkle to the economy.

The Landscape
Champagne sits cheek by jowl with the Paris basin on its western border and though the Aisne, Marne, Seine, Aube, and Yonne rivers flow through it, the landscape is generally arid and chalky. The east of Champagne borders with the industrial areas of Lorraine and the north with Belgium.

Agriculture, except in the Ardennes is mostly confined to the valleys. Wheat, cabbage and sugar beet are grown especially in the south where aromas emanating from the sugar refineries can be somewhat obtrusive.

Crests divide the plateau from northwest to southeast into several areas. In the east, bordering on Lorraine, is the largely agricultural so-called Champagne Humide (wet Champagne), and the Langres Plateau. In the centre is the Champagne Pouilleuse (Champagne badlands), a bleak and eroded plain, traditionally used for sheep grazing. Around these parts expect to see the odd run-down hamlet or two.

Troyes and Châlons-en-Champagne, Champagne's principal towns, are located in fertile valleys and are traditionally centres for the wool industry. A staggering 35% of all French woollen socks are produced here and Troyes in particular is famous for its factory shopping outlets.

A narrow strip along the westernmost crest of Champagne is extremely fertile, and the valleys around Reims and Epernay are the source of virtually all of the champagne produced in the area. These two areas are always competing to be the capital of Champagne, but who would dare argue with either.

Ardennes

Named after the Celtic word for 'deep forest', what Ardennes lacks in vineyards it makes up for in spectacular rivers, natural monuments and forested countryside.

Arduinna is the Celtic goddess who gave her name to the Ardennes mountains and indeed, the region. The word literally means 'deep forest'.

The wide-open lands of the Ardennes whose mountain mass is the oldest in Europe, are made up of dramatic valleys, deciduous forests and hills cut by the meanderings of the River Meuse, shared by their bordering neighbour in the north East - Belgium. That's why around the border limits, tourists will see both the French and Belgium flags flying proudly.

The panorama throughout the Meuse valley is very impressive. Some spots such as the **Roches la Dame** and **Roc de la Tour** have become designated view points for ramblers to help really take in the panoramic splendour.

The **Argonne forest**, where deer and boar are frequently hunted, is in the east. The central area is taken up with the peaks and pastures of **Ardennes Massif** where **Les Crètes pré-Ardennaises** dairy farms nestle in the countryside. A series of meadows of **La Thierache** are in the west and

---

Getting There:
From Calais take the A16 towards Dunkerque. At junction 8 take A26 for 126 miles. Then use the N51 for the final run.

Tourist Information:
Ardennes Tourist Board
24 place Ducale BP 419
08107 Charleville-Mézières
Tel: 00 33 (0)3 24 59 06 08
email: info@ardennes.com
www.ardennes.com

Ardennes

Ardennes

the southern area is mainly agricultural.

It is hard to believe that once upon a time, the calm and beauty bestowed by nature was so often bombarded by attacks especially by the Celts and then by the Romans and confounded by an assortment of kings and dukes over the last thousand years. So much so, that consequently, the region is dense with citadels and fortifications.

In the sixteenth century another war instigated by the

To really enjoy the area, follow a scenic tourist route. There are six routes to choose from and all are clearly signposted. These are:

☆ **The Fortifications Route** - a route taking in 2000 years of fortresses and citadels. It passes the fortress of Charlemont built by Charles Quint in Givet, Roman camp at Vireux and the Maginot Line - the last bastion of this fortification is in Villy-la-Ferté.

☆ **The Rimbaud-Verlaine Route** - follows the poets through towns that were important to these two poets from Charleville-Mézières where Rimbaud was born to Rethel where Verlaine was a teacher.

☆ **The Route of Legends of the Meuse & Semoy** - the river Meuse, the valley and its legends

☆ **The Route of the Fortified Churches of Thiérache** - a 150km route takes in fifteen fortified churches with keeps and watchtowers from Signy-Le-Petit to Signy-l'Abbaye.

☆ **The Porcien Route** - an 110km loop of hills, rural landscape and half timbered architecture of Ardennes taking in Rethel and Asfeld. In Asfeld there is a Baroque church in the shape of a viola.

☆ **The Forest, Lake and Abbey Route** - this route explores the forests, lakes, meadows and ponds so favoured with the monks before they were driven out during the Revolution. On route is Mouzon with its Gothic abbey built by the Benedictines in the 13th century. The tour passes through the Breval-Bois-Des-Dames forest where the celebrated 'Parc de Vision' is located.

Ardennes

Spanish Commander Francisco de Melo of the Army of Flanders, took place in **Rocroi**, a town located just two metres from the Belgian frontier. This event mobilised the inhabitants into making Rocroi, with the help of the military engineer Vauban, the most fortified town in northern Europe.

These fortifications are followed closely in grandeur by the 35,000m^2 **Citadel at Sedan** home to the largest mediaeval fortress in Europe. Sedan is also famous for its cloth manufacturing - a tradition dating back to the Middle Ages.

This flourished in the 16th century when after the Wars of Religion there was a sudden influx of Protestants. The lace stitch, brought in by the Calvinist community became known as the **Point of Sedan** by foreign buyers.

Givet, a town located at the very tip of Northern Ardennes also has its own fortress- the **Charlemont fortress** - on the banks of the Meuse river. It was named after its creator, Emperor Charles V, but was later redesigned by Vauban. It is accessible via a narrow road which stretches through the wood to the entrance of the military camp. These days the fortress is used for commando training.

The **Maginot Line** is another famous line of defence built to ward off the Germans. Constructed between 1929-40, the last bastion of this WWII fortification can be visited in **Villy-la-Ferté** (via N43).

Some remote villages without citadels, fortified their churches and the **Thiérache** has many of these amazing buildings.

The two world wars also saw battles fought in these parts, most notably the Battle of the Bulge in 1944.

> Did you know...
> That towns with no citadel or fortified castle opted to fortify their churches to have at least one building in their town or village which could offer them protection in the event of attack.

Ardennes Must Sees

Chateau Fort Citadel at Sedan
Reached via N43

The citadel, built on the site of a former 11the century monastery, covers a huge area of some 35,000m^2.

The twin towers and ramparts were constructed in 1424 and the bastions were added later in 1500s. Between 1642 and 1962, the fort was military owned but the town acquired it and restored it to its former glory.

Over its seven floors visitors can view life as the troops would have experienced it as everything has remained in tact.

A vision of a phantom recounts all the gory details of war and the history of France from 1424, the date of its construction, to May 1940 when the Germans circumvented the Maginot Line.

The twin towers display collections of medieval pottery, ceramics and the town's historical documents including a segment on the franco-Prussian War of 1870. There's also a great view over the town.

The Stronghold at Rocroi

Rocroi has the accolade of being the most fortified town in the region. The stronghold was built by Henri II in 1555 to counteract the threat from the Spanish held Charlemont fort in Givet. The stronghold benefited from the expertise of famous military engineer, Vauban. The present fortifications form a pentagon of streets which converge in a central square. A tourist trail starts at **Porte de France** and follows the east front which shows the complexity of the stronghold and its defence capability.

In 1643 a battle involving troops from France, Spain, Scotland, Germany and the Benelux countries was waged just 1km south of Rocroi, but France saw victory under the leadership of Duke Enghein, nicknamed 'Large Cop". Visit the **Musée de la Bataille de Rocroi** in the former guardhouse to see the battle reconstructed with tiny lead soldiers.

Ardennes Must Sees

Musée de la Forêt
Renwez
Tel: 00 33 (0)3 24 54 82 66
Reached via N43, near to Charleville Mézières

Tucked away in the Ardennes woods near the Belgian border is the unusual open air Forest Museum. The museum, opened in 1988, depicts the life and culture of woodcutters.

One hundred and thirty life size wooden figures, created by Henri Vastine are splitting wood, felling trees and doing the stuff that woodcutters do. Some are doing it with a two handled saw, some with an axe. Others are building fires.

On display are 3000 tools of the woodcutting trade and two steam engines.

Just across the border in Botasart, copycats have displayed their own wooden men. Naturally this has caused friction, but one thing is for sure, the originals are from Renwez.

Open daily.
By appointment in winter and on afternoons only in spring and autumn.
Entry 4 euros.

Musée Guerre et Paix
route de Sery
Novion-Porcien
Tel: 00 33 (0)3 24 72 69 50
Reached via D985

This museum is dedicated to three major wars that took place in the Ardennes between 1870- 1940.

Open daily. June-Sept 10am-7pm
Oct-May 10am-12noon.
Closed Tues
Entry 5 euros. Kids 3 euros

Parc de Vision Belval-Bois-Des Dames
Tel: 00 33 (0)3 24 30 01 86

This wildlife park in the heart of the Ardennaise forest of Belval, was created in 1967 as a haven for the indigenous animals that have lived here for centuries. It covers 350 hectares of wood, meadows and ponds but is out of bounds to humans. It is however, crossed by a 7km track with watchtowers so that visitors can observe the wild animals, such as boars, stags, deer bisons and bears enjoying life in semi-freedom.

Legends along the Meuse

The Meuse meanders through the deeply wooded forests of Ardennes where wild boars skirmish furtively and ancient legends thrive.

There is something both magical yet foreboding about the quiet of the forests of Ardennes. The Celts felt it and revered the trees with religious fervour. Ancient poets were inspired to concoct poems telling of legends about supernatural animals that supposedly lived there describing the forest full of tigers, elephants and dragons that were frightening enough to keep visitors away.

With so much folklore, when you hear a stirring or rustling of twigs today it could be a game bird, a boar or could it perhaps be a mythical pagan spirit or a 'nuton' (a sort of well dressed pixie)?

As the light trickles through the tree top canopies, all sorts of imaginings form in the mind's eye.

There is also the hypnotic sound of the constant flow of the river Meuse, meandering along ground flattened by years of water erosion with its twisty route well marked out into the ground heralding a village here or a legendary rock there.

Among the most well known are the **Dames de Meuse** (Women of the Meuse) - three gigantic rock said to be the petrified remains of three unfaithful women. But the most famous legend of all is the legend of the **Aymon** brothers and their trustee steed Bayart.

Rocher Des Quatre Fils Aymon
Rock of the 4 Aymon Brothers
Bogny-Sur-Meuse

This large 4 pointed quartz rock, on a loop on the Meuse represents the 4 celebrated cavaliers: the Aymon brothers, sons of the Duke of Aymon with their trustee horse Bayart, jumping over the Meuse river with the boys on his back.

Legends along the Meuse

The Aymon brothers had been knighted by the Emperor Charlemagne but legend has it that relations soured when one of the brothers, Renaut, killed Charlemagne's nephew over a disputed chess game. Of course Charlemagne sought revenge. The boys fled with the help of Maugis the wizard and their swift steed, Bayart, who could jump over large obstacles. When they were surrounded by Charlemagne's troops the horse leapt into action jumping across the cliffs to land safely on the other side of the Meuse River. They hid in the Castle-Regnault but Charlemagne found them. However, they fought so hard that Charlemagne finally gave up.

The Aymon Folk Festival
This is an annual festival held the first Saturday of August featuring live music, performed in the open air, by both local and national bands in the main square of Bogny-sur-Meuse.

Les Dames de Meuse
Laifur
Reached via D1 south of Laifour over a line of ridges There were three valiant kings, sons of the Lord Hierges called Héribrand, Geoffroy and Vauthier. Each married one of three blond virgins - daughters of the Lord of Rethel - called Hodierne, Berthes and Ige. The women promised the kings nothing less than eternal love. Sadly, their knights soon rode off to battle to join the crusades of Palestine with Goderoi de Bouillon. They stayed away so many years that finally seven years later the wives took lovers. On the night the crusaders took Jerusalem the Lord avenged them and changed the three women into three enormous schist rocks. You can see their dark masses rising 270m above the Meuse.

The area though awesome is still charming and is great for picnics especially by the riverside.

Legends along the Meuse

La Croix Scaille & La Tour Millénaire near Monthermé

The highest point in Ardennes is at La Croix Scalle. It is 504m/1654 feet high rising out of Thilay and stretches both the French and Belgium Ardennes. At the peak is the Millénaire tower. At 60m high it is an astonishing piece of work made of two reversed tripods. It is composed of six trunks of more than 40m connected by galvanized steel reinforcements with three floors arranged at 15m, 30m and 45m high. To reach these observatories, you must climb 233 steps to get to the top. The panoramas on offer are of the Ardennes forest over both Belgium and France showing off the local fauna and the flora.

<u>Getting there</u>: from Monthermé drive in the direction of Givet, at the Haut-Buttés crossroads take the direction of Neuville-aux Haies; follow the forest road of the Cross Scaille to the car park.
Open 11am-5.30pm at weekends and bank holidays weather allowing.
Entry is free.

Woinic - A Modern Legend? The World's Largest Pig
Bogny sur Meuse
Tel: 00 33 (0)3 24 32 03 54

Located 15km north of Charleville Mézières. It took the 21 year old Eric Sleziak 11 years and 12,000 hours of work to weld his pig together. It was finally completed in December 1993. Woinic weighs in at 56.5 tonnes which includes 6.5 tonnes of solder, and is 8m high, 14m long and 5m wide. Signs point you to the hanger where the pig resides. Sleziak still hangs around there. Feel free to ask him to show you around the metallurgical workshop. Contact him on the above number. There's no entry fee.

Givet

Givet, at the northernmost tip of the Ardennes is home to the Charelmont fortress and is a great lead into the Valley of the Meuse

Givet, located on the banks of the River Meuse, is known primarily for the Charlemont fortress, a citadel built in 1555 by and named after Emperor Charles V. On the west bank is the Givet St-Hilaire, a district centred around a church built by the 17th century military engineer Vauban. Victor Hugo was scathing about this church:

"the architect took a priest's or a barrister's hat, on this hat he placed an upturned salad bowl, on the base of the salad bowl he stood a sugar basin, on the sugar basin a bottle, on the bottle a sun partly inserted into the neck and finally on the sun he fixed a cock on a spit".

Givet has easy access onto the Meuse Valley via the N51. Passing the black marble quarries the road leads to the small village of **Hierges** featuring the ruins of an 11th-15th century castle. Turning right onto the D47 leads to **Molhain**, home to the **Ancienne Collégiale St Hermel**. This collegiate church was originally built over a 9th-10th century crypt.

Return onto the N51 towards **Vireux-Molhain**. This is a pleasant region at the confluence of the Meuse and Viroin. Archeologists have found a Gallo-Roman and medieval site on Mt Vireux. where you can still see a 14th century bread oven.

The meandering Meuse leads to **Fumay** famous for its blue slate quarries. This picturesque old town with delightfully twisting street nestles within a groove of the Meuse and is the capital of the **boudin blanc à l'oignon** sausage delicacy.

> **Getting There:**
> A26 for 126 miles. Then use the N51 for the final run.
>
> **Tourist Information:**
> 10 quai des Fours
> Tel: 00 33 (0)3 24 42 03 54

Charleville-Mézières

The two very different towns of Charleville and Mézières lying on the banks of the Meuse river merged in 1966 and formed the capital of the Ardennes region.

First there was the military town of **Mézières**. It was founded in the year 1000 as a humble village. In the 9th century it had become a fortified town. It is located in a peninsula encased in a loop off the Meuse river as if guarded by an almost complete circle of water. Its name derives from the Latin Maceriae which means - quite aptly - walls.

By the end of 16th century a citadel had been built to reinforce Mézières' strategic position which worked well for the town in 1815 when the Prussian advanced was arrested here for 45 days. In WWI the town was the headquarters of the German forces.

All that is left today of the heavy fortifications are some of the ramparts: the **porte of Bourgogne** and two towers: **La Tour du Roy** and **Tour Milart**. Mézières also has the **Basilica Notre-Dame de L'Espérance**, an excellent example of flamboyant Gothic style.

Charleville, a middle class city stretches along the north bank of the river and is overlooked by Mount Olympus. It started life as a Gallo-Roman

Getting There:
From Calais take the A16 towards Dunkerque. At junction 8 take A26 for 126 miles. Then use the N51 followed by the A34.

Tourist Information:
Ardennes Tourist Board
24 place Ducale BP 419
08107 Charleville-Mezieres
t: 00 33 (0)3 24 59 06 08
email: info@ardennes.com
www.ardennes.com
www.charleville-mezieres.net

Charleville-Mézières

city in the 5th century, which was destroyed by Barbarian invaders. It developed as a market town known as **Arches** and in the 9th century it acquired a royal palace.

It came into existence as Charleville centuries later in 1606 when it was founded by the Duke of Rethel, Charles de Gonzague (1580-1637) who named the town after himself. He gave the town trading rights in the 17th century attracting prosperity and wealth. There is a statue of him in Place Ducal.

The town is modelled on a symmetrical design centred around the elegant, gold stoned **Place Ducale** designed by Clément Métezeau (1581-1652). The square looks similar to place des Vosges in Paris attributed to Louis Métezeau

> Did you know ....
> that people from Charleville-Mézières are traditionally known as "Carolomacériens".

his brother. The centre piece of the square is a fountain and pink brick/ochre stoned arcades which frame the square, create an appealing effect. All four corners of the square are decorated with a dome and a public passageway (accessible when the museums are open) crosses the museum courtyard to link place Ducale with **place Winston-Churchill** where you will see the **Horloge du Grand Marionettiste**. This famous moving puppet clock has been designed into the facade of the Institut International de la Marionette. Every hour the head and eyes move by clockwork heralding a scene from a puppet show.

In 1966 these two towns merged to form the capital of Ardennes.

Markets in Charlesville-Mézières
Place Ducale
Every Tuesday, Thursday, Saturday, the square is alive with bustle and colour.

Charleville-Mézières

Arthur Rimbaud 1854-1891

The passionate, tortured poet Rimbaud was born in Charleville at 12 rue Bérégovoy south of Place Ducale and lived at 7 quai Rimbaud. His family were deserted by his father when he was seven, but he found no solace with his mother who was stiflingly conservative.

By the age of 17 he had already written his famous poem Le Bateau ivre. 1870 saw the Franco-Prussian war and he ran away from home to live as a vagabond. A year later he met Paul Verlaine with whom he had a tempestuous love affair. Together they travelled to London twice where Rimbaud began his famous prose poem A Season in Hell. The couple argued a lot and a quarrel that took place in Brussels ended with Verlaine shooting Rimbaud in the wrist. Verlaine subsequently went to jail for two years, and thereafter Rimbaud abandoned his poetry. He then embarked on a nomadic lifestyle in Europe and Africa where he explored, worked as a trader and even traded in arms. In1891 Rimbaud became afflicted with cancer in his right leg. There was no choice but to amputate but he died soon after. He is buried in Charleville-Mézière at the entrance of the old cemetery at avenue Charles Boutet.

Sketch of Rimbauld by Verlain whilst in Paris

His short career left an important legacy. He was a major symbolist poet and a major exponent of vers libre. His work influenced the surrealist poet André Breton and as well as the American song writers Bob Dylan and Jim Morrison. A bust of Rimbaud was erected in 1901 on Square de la Gare.

Paul Verlain 1844-1966

Paul Verlaine was a French poet and leader of the Symbolist movement in poetry. He was the son of an army officer and started his work life as a clerk and then became a civil servant. He married and had a son but a year later Verlaine met, fell in love and went to live with the young poet Arthur Rimbaud in Charleville. While serving an 18 month jail sentence for shooting Rimbaud, he wrote his finest piece: Romances Sans Paroles (1874). From 1877 he taught at the college of Rethel. He left this post in 1879 to run a farm with an adopted pupil Lucien Létitnois which failed. He ended his life living with prostitutes.

Charleville-Mézières Sights

Musée de la TSF
184 avenue Charles de Gaulle
Tel: 00 33 (0)3 24 56 12 41

A small but interesting museum housed in a former radio factory. It was in this factory that the first radio sets (Radio Ardennes brand) were manufactured from 1925 onwards. All aspects of the radio's evolution are methodically covered with documents, objects and old posters decade by decade.

Open daily 10am-12pm and 2pm-7pm except Tue, Sat and bank holidays
Entry and guided visits are free.

Basilica Notre-Dame D'Esperance de Mézière
Tel: 00 33 (0)324 57 53 92

The wonderfully flamboyant Gothic cathedral was built in 1499. It towers over Ardennes and at 154 metres high, is the tallest in the region. The church's moment of glory came when Charles IX married Elisabeth of Austria here in 1570. The original stained glass windows were destroyed in the world wars. Artist Rene Durrbach, an expert in the use of colour, created the windows you see now. The scenes are dedicated to the Black Virgin.

Open daily 9am-6pm Sunday 11am-1pm

Horloge du Grand Marionnettiste
Place Winston Churchill

This is a 12 metre wide monumental clock created by the famous monumental clock designer, Jacques Monestier. You will find it between the Ardennes museum and the International Puppet Institute. Every hour between 10am and 9pm the giant puppet, made of 6 tonnes of brass and copper plays out a scene of the tumultuous story of the four sons of Aymon: Ayman, Allard, Guichard and Richard and their horse Bayart who turned to stone in the Ardennes mountains. Giant hands stir the different protagonists into action. Catch the Saturday evening show at 9pm which presents all twelve scenes in succession.

Charleville-Mézières Sights

Le Mont Olympe
In the seventeenth century Le Mont-Olympe, was the site of one of the major fortresses in the citadel created by Charles de Gonzague to defend his city. Today its vast space houses an adventure playground, a marina, a nautical centre, a three star camp-site and a nautical base.

Musée de L'Ardenne
31 Place Ducale
Tel: 00 33 (0)324 32 44 69
The museum is housed in a series of buildings constructed between 17th-19th centuries connected by footbridges and covered passages. The museum is full of regional archaeology including illustrations of the first human settlements in the Ardennes spanning the Iron Age, the Roman times and the Merovingian period. For example there are displays of jewellery and arms found in the graves of Mézières'chieftans.

Other sections include history with relief maps, tools used by blacksmiths and slate-quarry workers and ethnography related to Charleville and the surrounding region.

There is also a Fine Arts section with displays of sculptures by Croisy (Four Seasons) and paintings by Couvelet, Gondrexon and Damas from the 19th century.
Open daily 10am-12pm and 2pm-6pm except Mon.
Free access for kids to 18 years

Note: One ticket costing 3,50 euros allows access to both Musée de l'Ardenne and Musée Rimbaud.

Musée Arthur-Rimbaud
Quai Rimbaud
Tel: 00 33 (0)324 32 44 65
Located at the foot of Mont Olympe (Mount Olympus) at the corner of the quay that carries his name, this museum pays homage to the famous poet Arthur Rimbaud. Behind the museum there is a footbridge which leads to Monte Olympus.
Open daily 10am-12pm and 2pm-6pm except Mon.
Free access for under 18s.

Charleville-Mézières Sights

A route to take from Place Ducal to the other sights

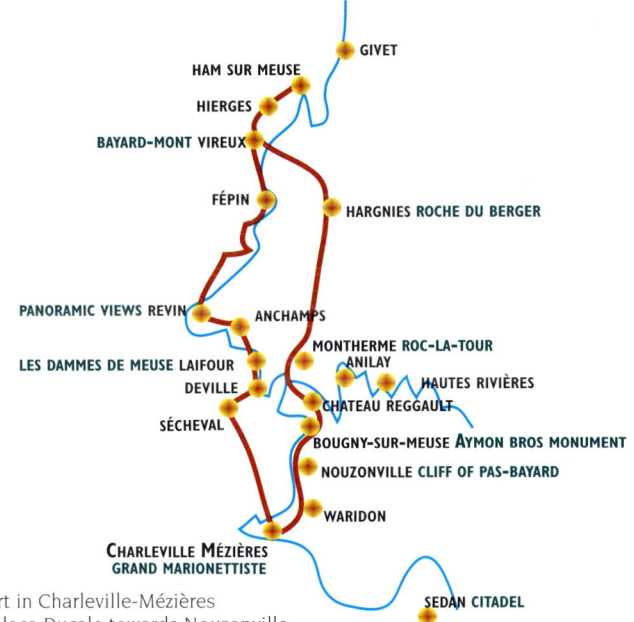

Start in Charleville-Mézières at place Ducale towards Nouzonville following the Meuse (by Waridon). At Nouzonville enjoy the cliff of the pas-Bayard. Next stop Bogny-sur-Meuse to see the Aymon brothers monument and the Poncin et Roche de l'Hermitage monuments. At Monthermé enjoy the view at Roc-la-Tour, and at Hargnies at roche du Berger (cliff of Herdsman) located in the forest before the village. Before Givet visit Hierges's castle and its beautiful village. In Vireux-Molhain's visit the Bayard-Mont and the Collègiate church. At Revin enjoy the view at Mont Malgrètout and at Laifour you will see the Dames de Meuse monument. Return to Charleville and visit the museum of Ardenne and the clock of Grand Marionnettiste (tall puppeteer).

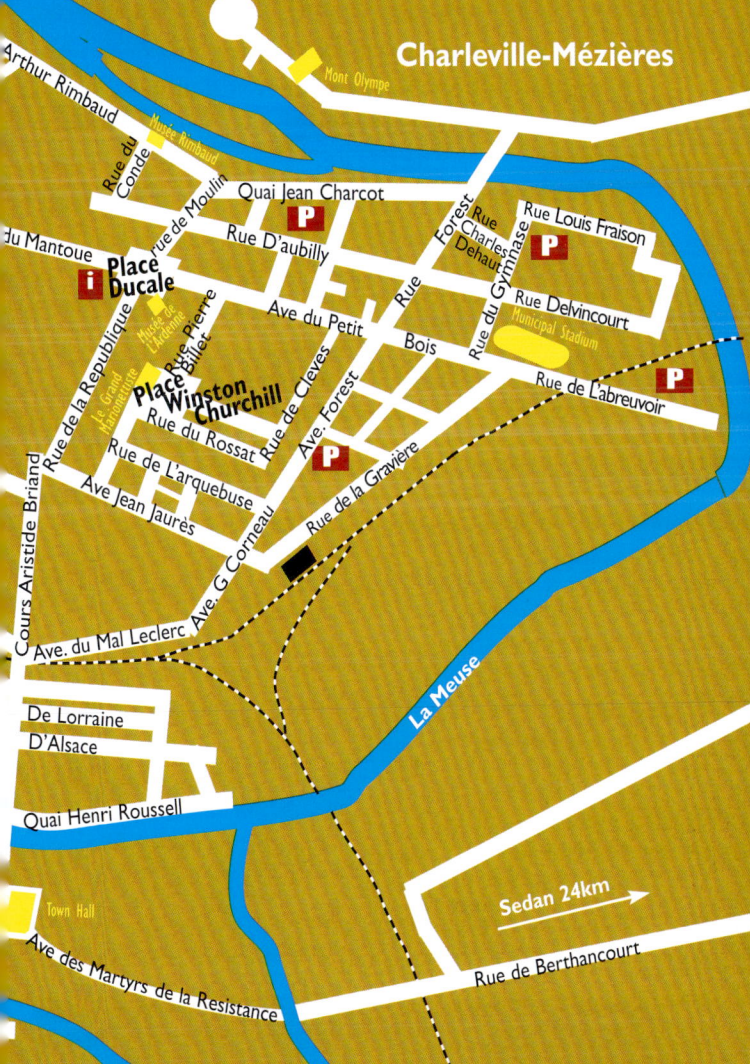

Marne

A region full of vineyard covered slopes deep forests and a huge historical heritage.

It's no surprise that in a region containing the two prestigious wine making towns of **Epernay** and **Reims**, the landscape is alive with vineyards, forests, rivers and lakes. Nature abounds and for those who love rambling, horse riding and the general feeling of being at one with nature, this region beckons.

It also gestures with an enticing finger at wine buffs who may find themselves too inebriated with the region to leave the **sacred Champagne triangle** which links Epernay, Reims and Châlons-en-Champagne, in any great hurry.

For a spiritual experience with a more cultural flavour, the Marne offers some truly magnificent churches and cathedrals, especially at Reims, **Tardenois** and **Sézanne** and the smaller villages around **Vitry-le-François**.

Marne is an area that made it into the military history books for the Battle of Marne. It took place in 1914 when Germans forced the French, led by Joseph Joffre, to retreat to a line along the River Seine but not before a bloody fight. *"The hour has come"* he wrote *"to advance at all costs and to die where you stand rather than give way"*. Though defeated, the battle was important as the French and British forces were able to prevent a swift German victory.

Getting There:
From Calais take the A16 towards Dunkerque. At junction 8 take A26 for 126 miles.

Tourist Information:
Marne Tourist Board
13 bis, rue Carnot BP74
Chalons-en-Champagne
Tel: 00 33 (0)3 26 68 37 52
www.tourisme-en-champagne.com

Marne

Forêt d'Argonne

**Two of the best kept secrets in Marne are its forest and its lake.
Nature and water sports abound.**

The Argonne Forest was the site of battle in World War I and it is still dotted with painful legacies. You may come across shell holes, trenches, cemeteries and numerous memorials that honour the soldiers who died in the fierce battles .

There are two chief towns in the area. The first is **Bar-Le-duc** (capital of the Meuse department) which is situated in the picturesque Ornain Valley. The town has managed to preserve its old houses, some dating back to the 16th century, and three ancient churches. It once was the capital of the county of Bar - a stretch of land reaching the Luxembourg border but it finally passed to the Duke of Lorraine and into French hands in 1766.

The second is the fortified town **Verdun** located on the Meuse river itself. It was here that the longest battle of World War I was fought in 1916 and where many monuments and a war museum can be found.

But those wending their way along the country roads will also come across petite, charming villages whose past religious faithful felt compelled to build churches that look somewhat oversized for the stature of the village.

The densely wooded forest itself sits between the plateaux of the Verdunois and the Champagne plains with Meuse river flowing along the plateaux. Every so often, steep cliffs and river valleys fringe the forest creating a deeply calming haven.

The forest is rich with fauna, flora and a great deal of animal activity. Indeed from October to March, the forest's lake, **the Lac du Der-Chantecoq,** (which incidentally, is the largest man-made lake in Europe) attracts bird watchers keen to observe the migrating birds who use this place as their refuge.

Epernay

Think Champagne and Epernay springs to mind. Take a stroll along Avenue du Champagne and it's easy to see why

You will find Epernay, the capital of Champagne, at the point where the **Côtes des Blancs** meets with the **Marne Valley** and the **Montagne de Reims**. Its well manicured hilly terrain and the chalk rock on which the town is built means the region is well endowed with the right sort of 'terroir' to make this a capital place for making its sublime nectar.

But the town was not always so elegant. Before the 5th century the region was a shamble of bramble marshes filled with sharp-edged spines. Then it was aptly called Sparnacun (from a Celtic word "sparn" meaning spine). Over the centuries all this changed and culminated with changing fortunes when in 1024 the city was passed into the hands of the Counts of Champagne.

The region is blessed with a magnificent setting and is strewn with vineyards and cellars devoted to champagne production. It makes hunting down your favourite tipple within the streets of this compact town a pleasure.

Streets to visit are **Avenue du Champagne**, **rue Mercier**, and **rue de Reims**, and all three stretch out from **place de la République**.

Many of the champagne houses can be visited. Refer to the Champagne House section which identifies those houses that accept visitors.

Getting There:
From Calais take A26/N51.
183 miles/294km

Tourist Information:
Epernay tourist office
7 avenue de Champagne
Tel: 03 26 53 33 00
www.epernay.net

Epernay Sights

Avenue du Champagne

The whole point of Epernay is to visit a champagne house. Take a stroll along **Avenue du Champagne** - this is no ordinary avenue. House after fabulous house of the greatest champagne producers, such as Moët et Chandon, Mercier, Vranken and Perrier-Jouet impress the landscape with their elegant Classic or Renaissance-style XIX century mansions. The avenue was classified in 1994 as a 'Site of Special Gastronomic Interest'. The houses straddle both sides of the avenue so you are spoilt for choice. Many houses are happy to receive visitors and detailed cellar tours end with a flute of champagne for a fee.

> Did you know..
> There are 90 million bottles of wine stored in 64 miles of underground cellars in Epernay.

Markets in Epernay

Clothes
Esplanade Charles de Gaulle
Sat 9am-6pm.

Food
Halle Saint Thibault
Wed-Sat 8am-12pm
Place Auban Moët
Sun am.

Notre Damme Church
Place Mendès-France

Though its architectural style was inspired by the 12th century Orbais church, Notre Damme was actually built between 1897 and 1917. The unmissable spire is 80m high. The bell in the belfry was provided by the ancient church of Saint-Martin and still regularly rings out an ancient ditty from 1491.

La Maison Gallice
33 avenue de Champagne

Finished in 1899 by the architect Charles Blondel, this magnificent building now houses the Office of Reginal Culture of Champagne-Ardenne. Inside the monumental staircase lights up the stained-glass windows created by Grüber in 1921.

Avenue du Marechal Foch
rue Des Sièges
rue du Général Sarrail
rue de la Chaude Ruelle
rue Leger Bertin
Place Carnat
Blvd du Cubry
rue Pasteur
rue de Sezanne
rue de Gallice
Avenue Paul Chandon
Place de l'Europe
Place des Arcades
Place Victor Hugo
Place H Plomb
rue de L'Hôpital Auben Moët
rue St Thibaut
rue St Martin
Place Auban Moet
Place Léon Bourgeois
rue des Berceaux
rue Eugene Mercier
rue Henri Martin
Eplanade Charles de Gaulle
rue Chandon Moet
Place de la Republique
rue Jean Moët
Achille Princier
Moët & Chandon
Place Mendes France
NOTRE DAMME CATHEDRAL
rue Pupin
Railway Station
rue de Janceline
Marne et Champagne
rue Moullin à Vent
rue Maurice Cerveaux
rue Joseph Vosage
rue de Bernon
Perrier Jouet
De Venoge
rue de Reims
Alfred Gratien
rue Croix de Bussy
Pol Roger
Vranken
Besserat de Bellefon
Esterlin
rue de Verdun
Demoiselle
rue Henry Le Large
Rue Roger Godart
Avenue du Champagne
rue d'alsace
Quai de L'ile Belon
Quai de la Villa
Marne River
rue de la Crayère
Avenue du Vercors
rue Charles Gounod
rue René Lemaire
Elizabeth Vollereux
rue de Metz
rue de Lorraine
De Castellane
Mercier
EPERNAY

Epernay Insights

Since its creation, the city has been destroyed more than 25 times. This explains why there are only two vestiges of the past : the Gate of Saint Martin and the frontage of the house of Louise of Savoy

Portail Saint-Martin
Place Hugues-Plomb

This monument, the oldest in Epernay, dates back to the sixteenth century and is all that remains of the ancient Notre-Dame church. It is decorated with garlands of stone and images of muscle men, various animals and a salamander.

Maison de Louise de Savoie
7 rue du docteur-Verron

If you happen to be passing, spend a moment to admire the exterior of this old library. It belonged to Louise de Savoie, the mother of François 1st. She loved the town and its champagne heritage. It was originally built in 1520 at **7 de la rue Flodoard** and burnt down in 1544.

Musée de la Cave et Des Metiers du Champagne
57 rue Verdun
Tel: 00 33 (0)326 51 19 11

The museum is located within the Castellane buildings whose tower dominates the town. There are two floors within the tower where visitors can admire the panoramic scenery of the Marne valley and the town of Epernay. Inside the museum are scenes illustrating the various stages of making champagne and artefacts from bygone days.
www.castellane.com
Open 25 Mar. to 31 Dec.
10-12pm and 2-6pm.
Entry: 3 euros.

Musée de la Tradition champenoise et de l'Imprimerie
57 rue Verdun
Tel: 00 33 (0)326 51 19 11

This is another initiative by Castellane which exhibits a rare range of printing machines. Included in the ensemble is a lithographic hand press.
www.castellane.com
Open daily 10-12pm and 2-6pm.

Reims

Famous for its champagne houses, Reims is one of the capitals of Champagne and certainly the most prestigious.

The city of Reims (locally pronounced R*annce*), is the official capital of Champagne. You will find it located at the confluence of the rivers Vesle and the Marne and is linked to Châlons-en-Champagne by a canal. Though not the most beautiful of Champagne's towns it does have the accolade of being one of France's earliest Christian towns thanks to Clovis who founded the bishopric in Reims. It was once the metropolis of Roman Belgica (which, incidentally, was the precursor to modern Belgium) and it was here in 496 that the warrior Clovis, was baptised St Remigius (aka St Rémi) and crowned thereby making him the only Christian ruler before the collapse of the Roman Empire.

Two hundred years later Louis I the Pious was crowned here endowing a religious character to the dynasty. Four hundred years later Louis VIII was also crowned here sealing its reputation as a place for coronations. A reluctant Charles VII (the Dauphin to Reims) was crowned on 17th July 1429 during the Hundred Years War with Joan of Arc in attendance. This feisty teenager inspired a sense of national identity into Charles and on her bidding he made his way to Reims and in doing so risked his life by crossing the hostile lands of Burgundy. A statue of Joan astride her horse faces the cathedral's Gothic exterior.

Getting There:
From Calais take the A16 towards Dunkerque. At junction 8 take A26 for 126 miles.

Tourist Information:
2 rue Guillaume-de-Machault
Tel: 03 26 47 25 69
www.reims-tourisme.com

Notre Dame Cathedral in Reims

Reims

By the time Charles X had come to the throne in 1824, no less than 25 kings had been crowned here at the town's most famous **Notre Dame Cathedral** and traditionally always on a Sunday morning. This regal event had the effect of endowing the wine of the area with the nick-name 'The King of Wines'.

It was around this time, when corks began to pop with the advent of sparkling wine, that Reims was beginning to find a new prosperity which continues to this day.

World War I obliterated the town but the cathedral remained unscathed and naturally became the city's focal point. In 1945 WWII was finally brought to an end in Reims when a document was signed in the technical college (**Salle de Reddition**) near the station marking the surrender of Germany.

The lattice work of cobbled streets and small alleys that make up the old town of Reims converge on the pedestrianised place **Drouet d'Erion**. This is where all the action is and where you will find its shopping arcades, cafes and restaurants.

As well as the historical 'must-see' sights there are ten or so champagne houses to tour within the city, four of which you can visit without an appointment including **Mumm**, **Piper-Heidsieck**, **Taittinger** and **Pommery**.

If you are not feeling too heady, enjoy a ramble through the town. Start at the **Porte Mars**, a splendid rusty yet still intact orange hued stone relic from the year 200. It is one of only four remaining from what was once the capital of the Roman province Belgica. This three-arched entry gate sits on a traffic island by two champagne houses. En route along the **Rue de Mars** you will see the lovely mosaic depicting the Champagne-making process on the building opposite the town hall. The **Cryptoportic**, a semi-underground Roman gallery is a little further on at **place du Forum**.

That should keep you busy before your next Champagne supping escapade.

Reims Sights

Two Images credit: Reims Office of tourism – M. Jolyot

Smiling Angel

Cathédrale Notre Dame
place du Cardinal-Lucon

The impressive Notre Dame is probably one of France's greatest cathedrals and considered a masterpiece of Gothic Art. Construction began in 1211 under the supervision of architect Jean d'Orbais and was finally completed almost 300 years later under Robert de Coucy.

It was built in the Lanceolate Gothic style achieving remarkable unity and harmony through the concerted effort of three architects: Jean Obray who contributed the choir and transepts, Jean Reims - the nave side of the west front and Bernard de Soissons. The west front has the superb world-famous 13th century sculpture of the Smiling Angel. You will find it in a splay of the north portal. The exterior has 2,300 statues and the gothic interior has high arches and vaults. So coveted is the local fizz that a stained -glass window depicts the production process.

The greatest achievement is to be found in the west end of the nave. Get there at the end of the afternoon when the sun lights up the two 13th century stained glass rose windows. Also admire the three windows painted by Chagall.

The Great War left the cathedral mostly undamaged and is maintained largely thanks to funds donated by the Rockefeller Foundation.

The cathedral, the setting for no less than twenty-five coronations, has been cited as a Unesco World Heritage Site

Reims Sights

and, probably, a contributory reason why the Champagne nectar has been dubbed 'Wine of Kings' and enjoys the global perception of superiority over other sparkling wines. In the square outside, where you would expect a tea room, a Champagne bar awaits.

Palais du Tau
2 place du Cardinal Luçon

This former palace of the bishops of Reims, dating back to 1690, was once the venue for post-coronation parties.

It was built by Mansart and Robert de Cotte and now houses some fine 15th century tapestries depicting the life of Clovis whose wife urged him to convert to Christianity. He refused, but one day while in deadly battle, the king prayed to God of Clothide for assistance. He won the battle and converted instantly.

The Tau is probably most famous for its statues. These

Palais du Tau

G H Mumm
rue de Savoye
Lanson
rue Camille
Ave Jean Jaures
rue de Cemay
rue des Mo
rue de l'Ecu
rue de Templiers
rue Werle
rue Kellerman
rue Coquebert
Cemetary
ruedi Cja,l de Mars
Krug
Boulevard Lundy
Pl. Aristide Briand
Boulevard de la Paix
Rousseau
rue Rogier
rue Voltaire
rue Ponsardin
Louis Roederer
Pl. Léon Bourgeois
rue Andrieux
Pl. du Boulingrin
rue du Temple
rue Jean Jacques
rue Coumeaux
rue C érès
Pl. Martyrs de la Resistance
rue A. France
Pl. Carnegie
rue du
Pl. de la Republique
Porte Mars
rue de Mars
Town Hall
rue de Général Sarail
rue Jacquin
Pl. du Ferum
Pl. Royal
rue Voltaire
Palais de Tau
Boulevard Joffre
rue F Roosevelt
Boulevard Foch
rue du Petit Four
rue Thiers
rue de Pouilly
rue des Elves
rue de Carnot
rue de Coucy
Pl. du C. Luçon
r d'Anjou
rue des Fuseliers
Cours J.B. Langlet
rue T Ducoudray
rue Roderfeller
rue des Telliers
rue du Clou dans le Fer
Pl. M Herrck
rue Chanzy
rue Brûlée
rue de Talleyrand
SNCF
rue des Capucins
Boulevard du Gl Leclerc
Boulevard Louis Roederer
rue
rue Clovis
rue Jean d'Arc
rue de Vesle
rue Libergier
Boul
Canal de L'
Boulevard M Noirot
A4 -E501 - A20 (E17)
Calais, Paris
Chausée Boce
Pa
Avenue de Paris
REIMS

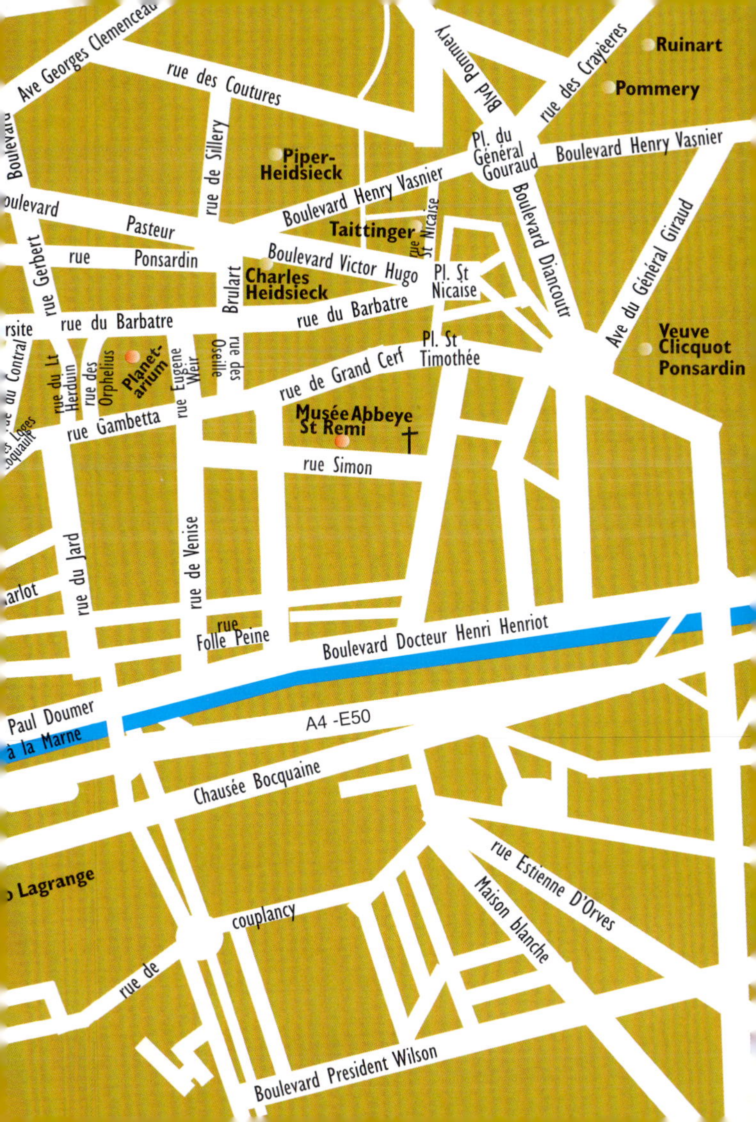
Ave Georges Clemenceau
rue des Coutures
Blvd Pommery
rue des Crayèeres
Ruinart
Pommery
Boulevard
rue de Sillery
Piper-Heidsieck
Pl. du Général Gouraud
Boulevard Henry Vasnier
Boulevard Henry Vasnier
oulevard Pasteur
rue St Nicaise
Taittinger
Boulevard Diancourt
Ave du Général Giraud
rue Gerbert
rue Ponsardin
Boulevard Victor Hugo
Brulart
Charles Heidsieck
Pl. St Nicaise
rue du Barbatre
rue du Barbatre
rsite
Veuve Clicquot Ponsardin
Pl. St Timothée
rue de Grand Cerf
rue des Oseille
rue Eugene Weir
Planet-arium
rue des Orphelius
rue du Lt Herduin
rue du Contral
Musée Abbeye St Remi
rue Gambetta
es Loges
oquault
rue Simon
rue de Venise
rue du Jard
arlot
rue Folle Peine
Boulevard Docteur Henri Henriot
Paul Doumer
à la Marne
A4 -E50
Chausée Bocquaine
rue Estienne D'Orves
Maison blanche
Lagrange
couplancy
rue de
Boulevard President Wilson

Reims Sights

include the Coronation of the Virgin (at the gable of the central doorway) and the monumental figures of St Paul and Goliath.

Basilique St-Rémi
place du Chanoine Ladame

The Basilique part of the former Benedictine Abbey is one of Reims' oldest buildings. It is where most early French kings were buried. It dates back to 1007 but little remains from its Romanesque or Carolingian beginnings.

Salle de Reddition
(World War II Surrender Room)
Collège technique de Reims
10 rue Franklin-Rosevelt

This was US General Eisenhower's HQ in 1945 and the place where the Germans signed their surrender.

Cryptoportique Gallo-Roman
place du Forum

In the third century AD Reims (known then as Durocortorum and changed by Ceasar to Civitas Remorum therby enshrining the name of the Remi tribe) was chosen by Ceasar to be the administrative centre of the Gallo-Roman times. Reims served as the capital of twelve cities and this matrix later served as the ecclesiastical order that followed in the middle ages. The most notable remains of the Roman Gallo era include the ancient Cryptoportique which lies beneath the present-day Forum of Reims. These are partly submerged Roman arcades which date back to 200 AD which many believe were used as a sort of Roman shopping centre. Access can be gained from mid June to mid September, Tues-Sun 2pm-6pm.

Rimbaud Museum
quai Arthur Rimbaud

The poet Rimbaud is thought by many to be one of the most talented symbolist poets. Born in Charleville he was writing poems in Latin by the time he

Reims Sights

was 14. At 17 he caused scandal with an affair with Paul Valeraine a symbolist writer and at 19 he gave up poetry preferring to travel and became a gun-runner. Meanwhile his poetry was to gain much recognition in his home country, but he didn't care. His knee injury meant the end of his activities and he died at just 37 years old. This museum is the story of his life.

Planetarium
Old College of the Jesuits
1 place Museux

If you like astronomy, this could be a peaceful retreat where the planets and night sky are the stars of the show.
Tel: 0033 (0)3 26 85 51 50

La Phare de Verzenay en Champagne
Le Phare de Verzenay
Musée de la Vigne
Verzenay

Located just 15km from Reims on probably one of the most prestigious slopes of the Montagne de Reims, this lighthouse is a fine monument to the vines of Champagne. A combination of audiovisual and cinematic displays makes this an entertaining education of how the wines of the region are made. Giant images and posters explain the subsoil and geology of the region alongside the history, the festivals and the lifestyle of the growers through the seasons.
Tel : 0033 (0)3 26 07 87 87
www.lepharedeverzenay.com
Entry: 6 euros
Open 10am-5pm.

Porte de Mars
Place de la République

This monumental arch is a relic from the second century Gallo-Romans times.

Châlons-en-Champagne & Beyond

The Mau and the Nau canals meander through Châlons en Champagne and a canal cruise is an ideal way to see the town.

Formerly known as Châlons-sur-marne, the town started life on an island in the Marne right at the heart of the chalklands of the Champagne region.

In Gallo-Roman times the city was referred to as **Catalaunum** after the Catalauni, a Gallic tribe who became Christians in 4AD. In June 451 the Romans defeated Attila the Hun's army around this area (the exact location remains unknown). It became known **Champs Catalauniques** and remained a symbol of their victory over the 'barbarians'.

The bishops arrived in the Middle Ages and the town's status rose to become an important administrative centre. During the Wars of Religion Châlon-en-Champagne remained loyal to the king while others joined the ranks of the Lique. So the town's status rose again when the king declared it to be the "main town of the Champagne region". Later in 1789 it developed into the main administrative town of the Marne region.

Though in its past, it was noted for its poverty, it is now applauded as a highly prosperous agricultural region. In fact it was here in 1749 that food preservation pioneer Nicolas Appert invented his system of preserving food by sterilisation.

The prosperity of the town is well illustrated through its

Getting There:
From Calais take A26/N51.
Located 50k from Reims

Tourist Information:
3 quai des Arts
Tel: 00 33 (0)3 26 65 17 89

Châlons-en-Champagne & Beyond

highly preserved half-timbered buildings, old large houses and the two old bridges spanning the Mau and Nau canals.

Two of the town's most appealing summer time features are the **boat trips** (catch one at 3 quai des Arts), bookable at the tourist office, along the canals which pass the old bridges and pretty gardens and the **Jard park** located on the banks of the Nau and affords a good view of the **Porte d'eau** of **Château du Marché** and its 16th century turret.

Jard park

The park is actually a former meadow on the bishop's estate, It was created in the 18th century with three distinct sections and crossed by the **avenue du Maréchal-Leclerc**. The **Petit Jard** is a Napoleon III style landscaped garden with a pretty flower clock where the ramparts used to be. The **Grand Jard** is a tree lined esplanade starting at the footbridge which links it to the Jardin Anglais over the canal and running along the River Marne. The Jardin Anglais, as the name implies is an English garden dating back to 1817, growing along the banks of the Marne Other must visits are:

Cathédrale St-Etienne

Building started in 1235 in the Lanceolate Gothic style which had been invented in Chartres 40 years earlier. Features include its Renaissance and medieval stained glass windows.

Eglise Notre-Dame-en-Vaux
5 place Notre Dame
Tel: 00 33 (0)3 26 65 63 17

This early Gothic church is considered a masterpiece of the Romanesque-Gothic transitory period. It features a noteworthy ambulatory that was inspired by St-Rémi in Reims, On the left of the church is the **Musée du Cloître de Notre-Dame-en-Vaux** which shelters sculptures of the old Romanesque cloisters.

Châlons-en-Champagne & Beyond

Rue de Chastillon
Take a walk along this road. Up to the end of the 1900s this road was called rue de la Basinerie and was where craftsmen had set up shop. Notice that the half-timbered buildings and buildings of note are on the even numbered side of the road. That is because the even numbered buildings were traditionally occupied by the well-to-do while the odd numbered buildings were where the manual workers resided. The building at number 2 is (quite aptly) where the Chambre of Commerce and Industrie is located. Its handsome gate dates back to the 16th century. Number 10 houses the regional chamber of commerce and numbers 14 and 16 are half timbered.

Notre-Dame de L'Epine
L'Epine
It is worth popping 8km/5miles further along the N3 to the next village of **L'Epine** to take a look at its 15th/16th century church. The village may be small but located in its heart is a grandiose Gothic church that thinks its is a Cathedral. It was, after all, modelled on St Remi Cathedral.

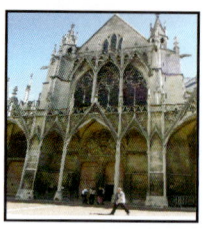

For hundreds of years the church - now a UNESCO world heritage site, has played host to pilgrims galore after shepherds discovered a statue of the virgin Mary in a burning thorn bush. The interior is Gothic in nature and the chancel is protected by an elegant 15th century rood screen and under the right-hand arcade is the 14th century statue of the Virgin Mary. One of the chapels houses a 16th century entombment.

It's facade is decorated in a flamboyant lace pattern with three doors and curious gargoyles protrude from various places each symbolising some medieval vice or other.

Sainte-Menehould

It is difficult not be curious about the place that saw the birth of the much revered Dom Pérignon. After-all this is the man that sold bubbles to the world

One thing is certain, Dom Pérignon's connection to this town certainly brings sparkle to an otherwise ordinarily pleasing holiday resort whose most attractive piece of architecture is the 18th century pink brick town hall in Place du Général-Leclerc.

However, the surrounding environment has huge appeal. The town is overlooked by a hillock known as 'Le Chateau' accessible by car via a ramp, then on foot through an alleyway and a flight of stairs. It has a prime position at the foot of the Argonne forest and many use Sainte Menehould as their base for trekking and rambling through the enticing forest.

The town got its name in the 15th century from Sigmar, counte of Perthes. He had several daughters the youngest of whom was called Manehould. She distinguished herself through her kindness and piety and so moved, her father named the town after her.

Gastronomically speaking, the town is also well known for its pig's trotters. Louis XVI was crazy about them. They are generally served in a very rich sauce but local restaurants generally add their own twist. Menu's offer them flambéed, boiled, cooked with vegetables or in wine, marinated in spices and herbs and even barbecued for forty hours so that the bones become crumbly.

> **Getting There:**
> From Calais take A26 to Reims, N44 then N3
>
> **Tourist Information:**
> 5 place du Général Leclerc
> Tel: 00 33 (0)3 26 60 85 83

Aube

The word "Aube" roughly means "dawn of a promising morning". Some say that waking up in the region does indeed hold promise of a great day ahead.

The Aube offers an abundance of vineyards and fine champagne houses to visit especially in the **Côte de Bar** region where a quarter of France's champagne production originates.

There are also the three man-made lakes and the natural park of the enchanting Orient Forest. These amazing features all combine to create 70,000 hectares of breathtaking countryside, a myriad of water and trekking activities and a fascinating dose of wildlife and bird watching.

The renowned factory shops of Troyes is a tradition that started in the sixties. These days there are over 150 shops and probably the most famous centres are Marque Avenue and McArthur Glen.

The area is also home to the fourth biggest theme park in France - **Nigloland**, a great venue within the **Foret d'Orient** for a family day out.

Renoir, one of France's most famous son's had a studio in **Essoyes**, a delightful village in the Aube and last, but not least is the delicious rose wine of the region - **Rosé des Riceys**. This rosé is so beloved in France that its production is one of the most controlled in France.

It is indeed a region with a lot of promise.

> **Getting There:**
> From Calais take the A16 towards Dunkerque. At junction 8 take A26 for 126 miles.
>
> **Tourist Information:**
> Aube en Champagne
> 34 quai Dampierre
> 1000 Troyes
> Tel: 00 33 (0)3 25 42 50 00
> www.aube-champagne.com
> bonjour@aube-champagne.com
>
> Nigloland 0033 (0)3 25 94 52

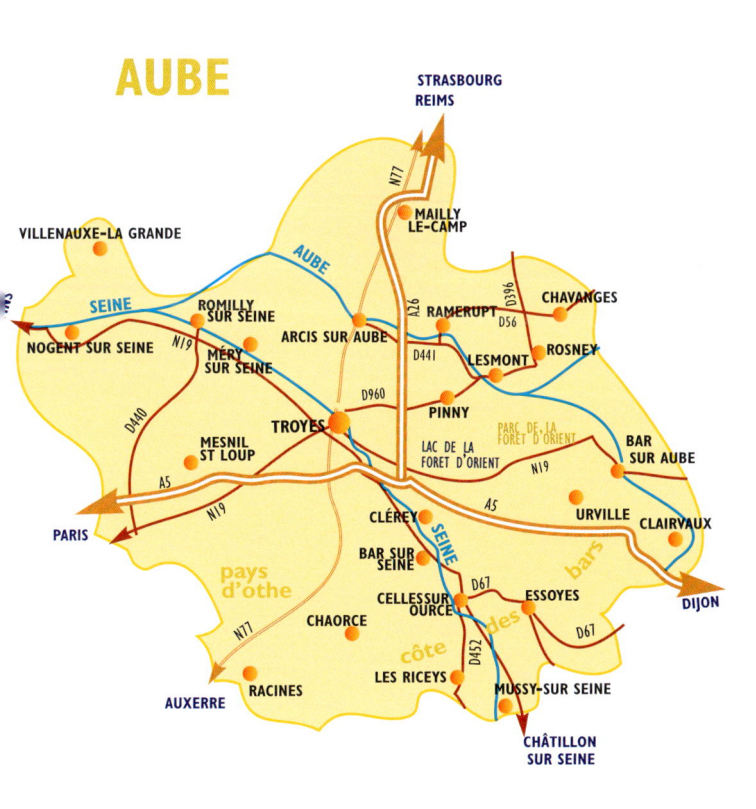

Aube

AUBE

Aube

Ancienne abbaye du Paraclet
Nogent-Sur-Seine
6km SE along N19 and D442
Héloïse & Abélard
A Doomed Love Affair

"You know, beloved, as the whole world knows, how much I have lost in you, how at one wretched stroke of fortune that supreme act of flagrant treachery robbed me of my very self in robbing me of you."
(Letter, Heloïse to Abelard)

Héloïse and Abélard, probably the most famous couples ever, were a pair of romantic lovers doomed to endure tragic separation.

Héloïse & Abélard depicted talking in a 13th century manuscript

It was in Paris that the great French philosopher Peter Abélard (1079-1142) and his pupil Héloïse (1101-1164) fell in love. She was a beauty, much loved by her uncle who ensured that she was the most educated woman of her time. She and Abélard bore a child, Astralab, and secretly married.

Héloïse's family were vengeful and after finding out about their secret marriage sent her to a convent and with the help of his servant, snuck up upon Abélard while he slept and castrated him.

Abélard went to the St-Denis abbey to become a monk and wrote 'Histoire de mes Malheurs' (History of my Troubles). His writing in general was regarded as controversial and he was eventually given leave to retire to the remote area of Le Paraclet in 1121. He built a modest oratory with reeds and straw but students flocked and helped to rebuild it in stone.

Ten years later Héloïse joined him and became the abbess of Le Paraclet in 1129. There is nothing left of the abbey except for a cellar located under farm buildings. However an obelisk marks the site of the crypt where Abélard and Héloïse were originally buried. Later, they were moved to the main church of Le Paraclet, but after the French revolution they were moved again to Père-Lachais Cemetery in Paris. Their tomb has become a pilgrimage site for sentimental lovers.

Aube Must See

Château de Chacenay Musée des Manuscrits
Tel: 00 33 3 25 38 79 46
1 rue du Château, Chacenay

Located in a remote wooded part of the Champagne countryside to the east of Bar-sur-Aube on the 'Route Touristique de Champagne' is this elegant medieval castle. The castle dates back to the 11th century with the colourful Gothic interiors. The history of Chacenay includes its very own Joan of Arc, Alix de Chacenay, who, attired in knight's armour valiantly fought in the Crusades

The castle is adorned with priceless art and artistic treasures and below in the 14th-century cellars are an extraordinary collection of manuscripts relating to people as disparate as Eiffel, Rasputin and Einstein.

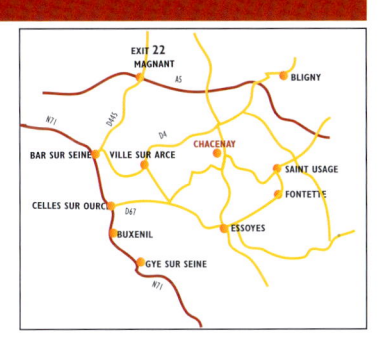

A 12th century chapel and a drawbridge with two towers lead to the Great Courtyard. The castle was the scene of many bloody battles, sieges and bombardments. It remained impregnable until it was conquered by Louis XI in 1472.

The castle also houses a magnificent collection of swords and guns that once belonged to the famous French General de Lignieres
www. chateaudechacenay. com
Open: daily from 1 June-30 Aug from 10.30am-12pm &2.30pm-6.30pm.
Entry: 8 euros for adults
6 euros for kids to 16 years.

Les Riceys

Les Riceys is the largest wine growing region of Champagne with an impressive 866 "Appellation" vineyards

The picturesque town of Les Riceys is actually a commune of three small market towns. Some may note a distinct Burgundian feel to the commune and that is due somewhat to its history.

Until the Revolution the three towns were at times within the County of Champagne and at other times within the Duchy of Burgundy and not necessarily all at the same time either as a consequence of conquest or nuptials. But throughout its history, the vineyards, whatever their nationality, thrived.

With so many appellation vineyards perhaps it is not so surprising that Les Riceys is the only commune in France to have as many as three registered 'Appellations d'origine Controllée' wines. In effect, the quality of the wines have to undergo stringent quality checks before it reaches your palate. These wines are 'champagne,' coteaux champenois' and 'rosé des Riceys'. The rosé des Riceys even has its own cult following of locals who love its full bodied and intensely fruity flavours. Even Louis XIV succumbed to it its charms.

As the measures in place to ensure quality are so severe, it is not possible to guarantee that the wine will be produced every year. Only one grape is used - Pinot Noir- and then only those plucked from the steepest and sunniest slopes and then only in dry weather.

Getting There:
From Troyes take the N71

Tourist Office:
3 place des Héros de la Résistance
Tel: 00 33 (0)325 29 15 38
www.les-riceys-champagne.com

Les Riceys

Vineyards in Les Riceys to visit and taste Rosé des Riceys

Guy de Forez - Ricey Haut
32 bis rue du Général Leclerc
Tel: 00 33 (0)325 29 98 73
Housed in a beautiful building with XVII cellars and a traditional press. Guided tour in English and tasting.
Costs: 3 euros

Morel Père et Fils
Ricey Haut
93 rue du Général de Gaulle
Tel: 00 33 (0)325 29 10 88
Five generations of growers have been here. Detailed guided tours include demonstrations, a tour of the vaulted cellars and village and ending in a tasting.

Cost : 5 euros

Morize Père et Fils
Ricey Haut
122 rue du Général de Gaulle
Tel: 00 33 (0)325 29 30 02
Guided tours and tasting costs 3 euros.

Gallimard Père et Fils
Ricey Haut
18/20 rue Gaston Checq - Le Magny
T**el:** 00 33 (0)325 29 32 44
Tour and tasting in English
Cost: 3.05 euros

Jacques Defrance
Ricey bas
24 rue Plante Bas
Tel: 00 33 (0)325 29 32 20
Guided tours include tour of the village and tasting.
Cost: 3 euros

René Bauser
Ricey Haut
Route de Tonnerre
Le Magny
Tel: 00 33 (0)325 29 32 92
Free guided tours.
English spoken

Forêt d'Orient & The Great Lakes

Preservation of the varied countryside and its large open spaces, means visitors have a patchwork of environments to enjoy

The Forêt d'Orient Regional Park, lying 10km just east of Troyes, was chartered as recently as 1970 and encompasses an area of 71,489 ha, gathering together 50 communes and 20,000 inhabitants. The highly preserved regional park is made up of a natural patchwork of landscapes consisting of **Champagne Crayeuse** in the northwest, **Côtes des Bars,** made up of plateaus and river

---

The Foret d'Orent, located about 16km east of Troyes, has the largest artifical lakes in Europe.

Get There: Reach it from N19 where at Lusigny a minor road takes the western shore to the D1 and west into Geraudot. You can take the D43 from here along the northern edge. It continues to the eastern side of the lake to the marina at Mesnil-St-Pere.

Lac Amance: ideal for jet skiing and watersports.

Lac du Temple ideal for wildlife and fishing.

Lac d'Orient: has fine sandy beaches at Plage de Geraudot and along the wooded shoreline. It is ideal for saling and swimming.

Forêt d'Orient & The Great Lakes

valleys in the south east, **Vallée de L'Aube, Plaine de Brienne** where riverside forests border on remarkable orchid patches and in the centre is the **Champagne Humide** with its waterlogged rolling hills and indefinable charm.

Nevertheless, the region began its beautification as far back as the 13th century when the Knights Templars and Knights Hospitallers of the Kingdom of Jerusalem settled in the **massif**. With them came expertise in agriculture, forestry, mining, fish raising, and some fish raising ponds, such as the Forêt de Temple, and Fôret d'Orient which still exist.

The Order had the monopoly on the forest's resources and guarded this jealously. They built damns and drills in what was a quasi inaccessible forest specifically to maintain the marshy character of the forest throughout the year to ward off unwanted visitors exploiting of the wood.

They undoubtedly succeeded and to this day, even with the short cuts and signs the forest remains difficult to reach and ramblers will see countless dams dotted around.

The heart of the area is Europe's largest man-made reservoir, Lac d'Orient as well as two small lakes known as Lac de la Temple and Lac d'Amance, all three of which were built to regulate the flow of the Seine and the Aube and

Tourist Information:
Office de Tourisme Intercommunal
Maison du Parc, 10220 Piney
Tel: 00 33 (0)3 25 43 38 88
www.pnr-foret-orient.fr

Forêt d'Orient & The Great Lakes

to provide water for the Paris area.

Further north east is the **lac du Der Chantecoq**. They have become rich yet fragile ecosystems and fabulous woodland and farmland areas and hedgerows surround the lakes making these perfect habitat for breeding birds. These lakes are very popular with water sport lovers, hikers and especially bird watchers who may catch sightings of cranes on migration and over-wintering, local species such as the white tailed eagle, buzzard, mallard and bean goose.

There are also a number of campsites that border the lakes of Southern Champagne so those inclined to do so can really get up close to nature. The Site du Chantecoq has an observation hideout and a birdlife museum. The most convenient campsite is located at in the little town of Dienville right opposite Lac Amance's Port Dienville.

MUST SEES

Maison du Parc, 10220 Piney
Tel: 00 33 (0)325 43 81 90
The tourist information office and a museum is housed in an ancient farm and contributes to the activities and development, both natural and scientific, of the region. The ground floor evokes the life of the region through the sun, water and the forest. The first floor shows off the amenities of the area including activities.
<u>Getting there</u>: It is on periphery road of Lac de la Forêt d'Orient at the junction of CD79 and CD43.
Open all day in January, February, March, November and December except bank holidays. Open 1pm-5pm In April, May, June, September and October.

The Animal Park
Situated on an 89ha peninsula near the Lac d'Orient, between Mesnil - St.- Père and the Maison du Park, this specially adapted park is populated by stags, roedeers and wild boars all living in semi-freedom. Armed with binoculars and patience you will be able to observe the animals from two watchtowers located on the borders of the wood.

Typical timbered building in Troyes

Troyes

Probably the most charming Champanoise town, Troyes is a wonderfully romantic composition of wood and stone.

Troyes is a gem of a medieval town located in the north east of Champagne on the banks of the river Siene. It may be small in size, but it is big in stature, long in rich history and peppered with countless accolades.

Originally the town was known as Tricasses in the 1st century after the Celtic tribe that had settled there. It then became Augustobona, a Gallo-Roman city named after the Roman emperor Auguste. By the 3rd century during the barbarian invasions it changed its name to Tricassium and in the 5th century it changed again to Trecae. By the 10th century Troyes became the capital of the county of Champagne.

The town was renamed after the Greek town of Troy whose people fled after the war over Helen of Troy. The Trojans founded settlements all over Europe, including Troyes, bringing with them their traditions, including the building of mazes. The lattice-work of tall narrow streets and bendlets is probably an evocation of this.

In 878 Louis the Stammerer received the imperial crown from Pope John VII in St Jean's Church but by 956 the first Count of Champagne, Robert "the very glorious Count of

> **Getting There:**
> All the following roads lead to Troyes:
> RN17, RN77, A5, A26
>
> **Tourist Information:**
> Troyes Office of Tourism
> 16 Carnot Boulevard
> Tel: 00 (0)3 25 82 62 70
> email: troyes@club-internet.fr
> www.ct.ot-troyes.fr

Troyes

Champagne" ruled over the city. It was the counts who promoted the expansion of the city and the Champagne fairs became famous. The counts of Champagne chose Troyes as their capital and for two hundreds years it flourished as a commercial centre. During this golden age traders came from all around to participate in the fairs that took place during July, August and November. The counts began to fortify the town with ramparts, a task finally completed in 1222 when Thibaut IV finished building the ramparts and gave it its final cork shape.

A marital union at end of the 13th century meant that Champagne became part of the Kingdom of France.

In 1420 The Treaty of Troyes, was signed in the town sworn by Charles VI and Henri V in Troyes Cathedral finally settling the Hundred years war.

Troyes' many accolades include being the most densely populated with 16th century timbered architecture in Europe (despite the many fires that destroyed much of the buildings). Many of these fine buildings are found south of the central main shopping street in **rue Emile-Zola** and around the cathedral and in the alleyways of the old town off the pedestrianised **rue Champeaux**.

The city is also home to ten churches, 8 of which are listed buildings and renowned as a

Troyes' is shaped like a cork

> Did you know...
> that, by happy coincidence, the town of Troyes is shaped like a cork. Some even say that it is aptly shaped like a sock in tune with Troyes hoisery industry.

Troyes

> Did you know...
> The typically medieval street rue or ruelle des Chats was so named because the gables of the houses were so close together that their roofs almost touched allowing cats to jump from one attic to another with some ease.

Chrétien de Troyes
Have you ever wondered how the French have become so associated with chivalry? In all probability this perception was created by the French poet Chrétien de Troyes when he conveyed this impression through his romantic writing and poetry. He was an immensely gifted poet and the French language owes him so much. Chrétien drew on popular legend and history, and imbued his romances with the ideals of chivalry current at the 12th-century court of Marie de Champagne, to which he was attached.

He was the author of the first great literary treatment of the Arthurian legend. Other works include imitations of Ovid and Guillaume d'Angleterre
His narrative romances, composed c.1170-c.1185 in octosyllabic rhymed couplets, include Érec et Énide; Cligès; Lancelot, le chevalier de la charette; Yvain, le chevalier au lion; and Perceval.

historic centres for stained glass windows and honoured with the title of "Holy city of stained glass".

Contrastingly the synagogue on **rue Brunnval** was inaugurated in memory of the Jewish scholar Rachi (1040-1105) in 1987. He was a member of a small Jewish community which flourished for a time under the protection of the counts of Champagne. His commentaries on the Old Testament and Talmud are still revered by academics today. The Rachi University Institute facing the synagogue is devoted to the study of his work.

The city is also famous as capital for hosiery and garment making industry. This last accolade was a result of Louis XIII's unkind decree that charitable houses had to be

Troyes - Factory Shopping Outlets

> Did you know...
> If you put all the stained glass windows of all the local churches of Troyes together you will achieve a massive surface area of 9000 square metres.

self-supporting and self-financing. Undeterred, the entrepreneurial spirit took hold at the orphanage of the **Hôpital de la Trinité** and they set about knitting and selling stockings.

Shoppers still flock to Troyes to take advantage of the discounts at the factory shops that have congregated there offering quality wares at lower prices. After all who can resist a bargain!

FACTORY SHOPPING OUTLETS

McArthur Glen Troyes
Pont Ste-Marie
Tel: 00 33 (0)325 70 47 10
www.mcarthurglen.fr
There are 84 factory shops here including Black & Decker.
Open:
Monday to Friday 10am-7pm
Saturday 9.30am-7pm
Get there:
Take the A4 then A26. Take exit 22 following signs to Charmont Barbuise/Port Sainte Marie. Then follow signs for Troyes/Pont Sainte Marie.

Marques Avenue
114 bd de Dijon
10800 St Julien les Villas
Tel: 00 33 (0)325 82 80 80
www.marquesavenue.com/troyes
This shopping outlet has a dazzling 240 shops
Open:
Monday 2pm-7pm
Tuesday-Friday 10am-7pm
Saturday 9.30am-7pm
Get there:
Take the A26 motorway and follow the A5. Take exit 21 sign-posted Troyes/St Thibault, then follow signs to Troyes/St Julien Villas

Troyes - Speciality Shops

Escapade Gastronomique en Champagne-Ardenne
61 rue de la Cité
Tel: 00 33 (0)325 80 97 41
Just steps from the Cathedral is this great **gastronomic** shop. On offer are over 300 diverse speciality dishes from the Champagne-Ardenne region. Examples are the boudin-blanc from Rethel, biscuits rose from Reims, foie gras Champagne style, Chaorce the regional cheese and beer from Vlamy.

Aux Crieurs de Vines
Les halles de l'Hotel de Ville
Tel: 00 33 (0)325 41 01 01
There are 300 varieties of **wines** on offer including regional examples and champagnes. There's also a bar to try before you buy.

Markets in Troyes
Marché des Halles
Mon. to Thur. 8am-12.45pm & 3.30-7pm.
Fri. & Sat. 7am-7pm
Sun. 9am-12.3-pm

Le Palais du Chocolate
2 rue de la Monnaie
Tel: 00 33 (0)325 73 35 73
Love **chocolate**, love this world class chocolate shop - Pascal Caffert has won trophies for his chocs. He makes them with almonds, beer, strawberries, lemons and passion fruit, whisky, champagne and even without sugar. Is there no end to this man's talents? He likens chocolates to wines in that cocoa varieties do matter to the quality of the chocolate.

J-P Gerard
42 rue Emile-Zola
Tel: 00 33 (0)325 73 09 95
This shop is regarded as the best **boulangerie (bakery)** in the city. Try from 20 types of bread ranging from cereal to organic. Great cakes too.

Jean-Pierre Ozeree
Halles de l'hotel de ville
Tel: 00 33 (0)325 73 72 25
This speciality **cheese** shop is run by the Ozerees who delight in telling you how to serve and store their cheeses.

Troyes Sights

The Museum of Modern Art
Place Saint-Pierre
Tel: 00 33(0)325 76 26 80

This amazing museum, located next to the cathedral within the sumptuous surroundings of the episcopal palace, is the pearl of cultural Troyes. An art loving couple, Denise and Pierre Lévy donated 2000 masterpieces to the museum in 1976. This collection is unique and includes Braque, De Vlaminkc and mostly Derain including his famous paintings of Big Ben, and Hyde Park. Later friends of the famous artist André Derain, donated a further 80 paintings, 52 drawings and 77 sculptures that the artist had created. The collection is continually expanding as more contemporary art joins the collection. Also on show is a prestigious display of ancient African sculptures and crystal glasses by Maurice Marinot, one of the key figures in reviving the art of glass in France at the beginning of the 20th century.
Open: 11am-6pm daily except Mon. and bank holidays
Entry: Free on Wed.and the first Sun. of the month.

The Tool Museum
7 rue de la Trinité
Tel: 00 33 (0)325 73 28 26

The Tool Museum - **Maison de l'Outil** - displays 8,000 18th century hand tools used on wood, iron, stone, leather and thatch in a 16th century courtyard house. The building was originally owned by the wealthy Mauroy family but, not having any children, let it be used as an orphanage 'L'Hôpital de la Trinité'. Children were fed, educated and taught to spin cotton. When Louis XIII decreed that houses depending on charity should be self sufficient, the "Manufacture de la Trinité soon became the largest hosiery in Troyes. It had to close down in 1792 due to the French Revolution. The building was bought by the town in 1966 and given to "Compagnons du Devoire" who have historical routes dating back to the Middle Ages. The collection was put together by them.
www.maison-de-l-outil.com
Open: 10am-6pm daily
Entry: 6 euros, kids Free

TROYES

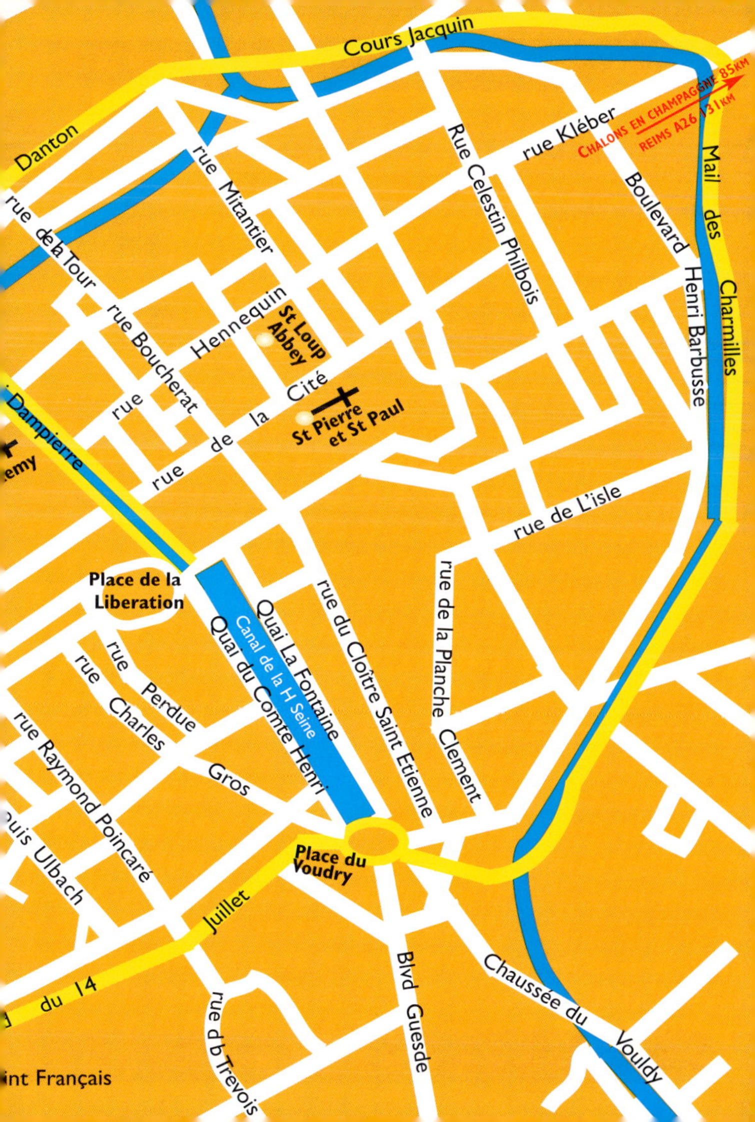

Cours Jacquin
Danton
CHALONS EN CHAMPAGNE 85KM
REIMS A26 131KM
rue Kléber
Rue Celestin Philbois
Boulevard Henri Barbusse
Mail des Charmilles
rue Mitantier
rue de la Tour
rue Boucherat
Hennequin
St Loup Abbey
rue de la Cité
St Pierre et St Paul
rue
Dampierre
rue de L'isle
Place de la Liberation
Canal de la H Seine
Quai La Fontaine
Quai du Comte Henri
rue du Cloître Saint Etienne
rue de la Planche Clement
rue Perdue
rue Charles Gros
rue Raymond Poincaré
Louis Ulbach
Place du Voudry
Juillet
du 14
Blvd Guesde
Chaussée du Vouldy
rue d b Trevois
int Français

Troyes Sights

Ste-Madeleine Church
rue Ste-Madeleine

This church, the oldest in the city has a rare delicate stonework rood screen (jubé) made by Jean Gailde whose purpose is to keep the priest separate from the congregation. Amazingly the scalloped arches have no apparent means of support. Also worth viewing is the statue of St Martha.

Open: Free access all year except Sun. morning.

Musée Saint-Loup et d'Histoire Naturelle
rue Chrétien-de-Troyes
Tel: 00 33 (0)25 76 21 68

Located a few steps from the cathedral, this natural history museum contains a remarkable assortments of archeological artefacts. Items include regional fauna such as birds, geological displays and a variety of fossils. Next to it is the Musée des Beaux-Arts, with its ensemble of pictures from major European schools from 10th century to date. Other items include medieval sculptures.

Open: daily 10-12pm and 2pm-6pm except Tues & bank holidays

Château de Cirey
Cirey sur Blaise
Tel: 00 33 (0)3 25 55 43 04

Though not in Troyes, a detour to Cirey sur Blaise on the N67 or D2 roads may well be worth it to see the former residence of Voltaire (1694-1779) - a man considered to be the embodiment of 18th century enlightenment.

The château, located near to the Blaise river, was his home for 13 years when he co-habited with his married lover Emille. Bizarrely, it was Emille's husband that actually owned it. The Château evokes a wonderful ambience depicting his time there.

Inside, located in the attic, there is the Little Theatre, built in 1735 which was designed by Voltaire himself after the failure of his play 'Semiramis' in Paris. The theatre is one of the few examples of early French theatres.

More information: www.visitvoltaire.com

Essoyes - Renoir's Garden

Essoyes has two accolades: the revered vineyards and the legacy of impressionist painter August-Renoir.

Auguste-Renoir
1841-1919

This pretty, peaceful village just south of Troyes is located on the edge of the Ource river. Renoir married a local called Aline Charigot, and became so enchanted with the beauty, the light, the landscape, lifestyle and countryside of the region that he settled here in 1895. By 1905 he had built his workshop. Today the Renoir Association, founded in 1986 by his grandson Claude Renoir, aims to foster the work of young professionals. A competition is held and the winner receives a scholarship and lodging in Essoyes for a year. At the end of the year, the artist's works is exhibited in the village in the Champagne House **Veuve Devauxe**, a partner of the Renoir association.

There are four signposted Renoir paths through the village. These lead to hot spots that inspired Renoir's masterpieces

Atelier Auguste-Renoir
Renoir's Studio
7 rue Extra, Essoyes
Tel: 00 33 (0)3 25 38 56 38

Renoir spent 25 summers here creating his masterpieces on the second floor of this small stone building at the bottom of his garden. You can still see his easel and chair and the paint he dropped on the wood floor. In later years he hands became deformed with rheumatism and the brushes were taped to his wrist. On the ground floor there is a bookshop where prints are sold. His ancestors still live in the house he and his wife **Aline Charigot** (a local of the area who he met in Paris and who became his model then wife) enjoyed. You can also visit the couple's graves in the nearby cemetry. Bronzes of Renoir and Aline, made by him, grace the monument.

Open 2pm-6.30pm from 30 Apr. to 16 Sept.

Essoyes - Renoir's Garden

which in turn served to immortalise the scenery. These spots are marked with a print of the masterpiece reproduced on stone, complete with ease,l so you can compare the view with the painting. Routes start at the Essoyes town hall at the signpost marked 'I".

Chemin Montant dans les Hautes Herbes.
(3km 45 min)(Path of the rising grassy regions). This region inspired the work opposite, of the same name in 1875. The original is currently on show in Paris.

Aline Charigot Route
(7km 1 hr 45 mins)

Pierre-August Renoir Route.
(12km 3 hrs)
This route takes in the hillside vines, the stone huts (cadoles) and tree lined avenues. Renoir's painting "Vue de Essoyes" is pictured here.

Route Gabrielle Renard
(14km, 3 hrs 30mins)
Along the routes there are six different masterpiece reproductions to view:

Map
Ref Painting
1. Route de Loches
2. Les Laveuses
3 L'église d'Essoyes
4 Chemin montant dans les hautes herbes
5. Gabrielle au jardin
6. Square Gabrielle

Also Worth Visiting

Maison de la Vigne
House of the Vine
9, Place de la Mairie
10360 Essoyes
Tel: 00 33 (0)3 25 29 64 64
The world of the vine in Champagne and the life of the vine growers is illustrated through tools of the trade, old and new techniques and images. Some of Renoir's prints are on display. Tours include a visit to the cellars and there are wine tasting opportunities and tips for those interested in learning about oenology and the finer points of wine tasting
Open daily 2.30pm-6.30pm

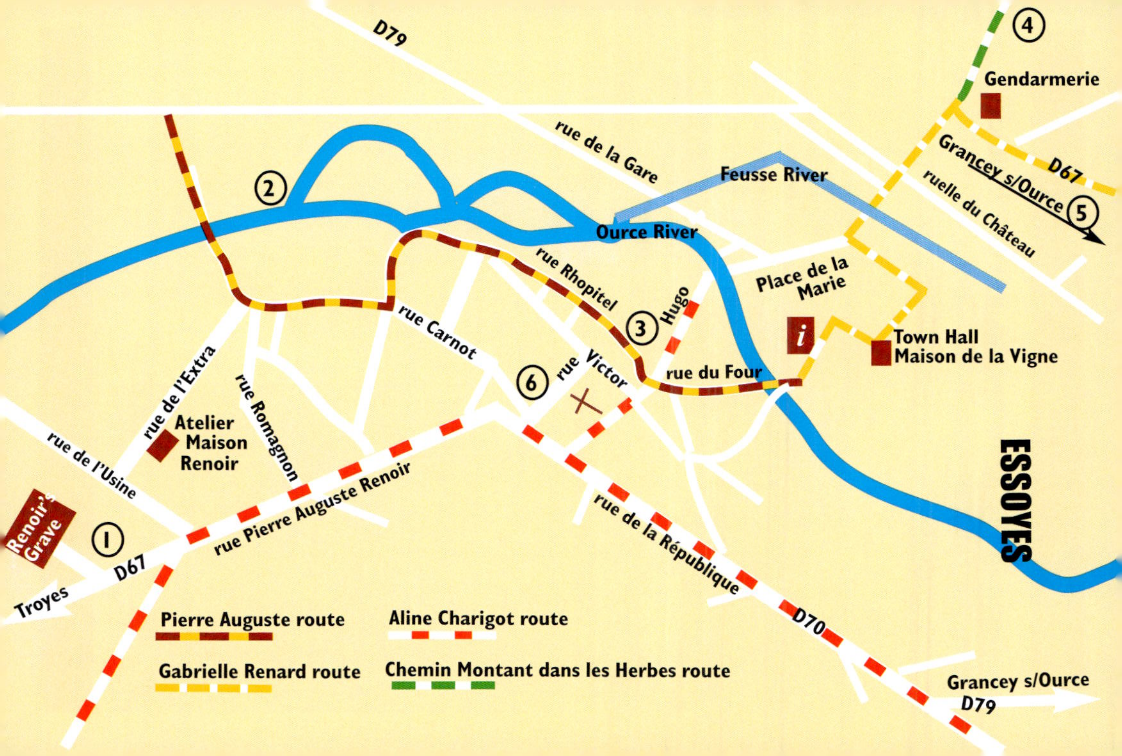
ESSOYES
D79
rue de la Gare
Feusse River
Ourse River
Gendarmerie
Grancey s/Ource
D67
ruelle du Château
Place de la Marie
Town Hall
Maison de la Vigne
rue Rhopitel
Hugo
rue Victor
rue du Four
rue Carnot
rue de l'Extra
rue Romagnon
Atelier Maison Renoir
rue de l'Usine
Renoir's Grave
Troyes
rue Pierre Auguste Renoir
rue de la République
D70
Grancey s/Ource
D79
Pierre Auguste route
Gabrielle Renard route
Aline Charigot route
Chemin Montant dans les Herbes route

Chaource - The Town

Deep in the heart of "Champagne Humide" lies the town of Chaource, whose local cheese, graces many gastronomic tables

The town's curious name is the union of the two French words 'chat' (meaning cat) and l'ours (meaning bear) both of which appear on the town's coat of arms.

Chaource is a town of the Middle Ages and its roads are still lined with 15th century houses. However, it is most famous for the full fat cheese it produces of the same name, (refer to Eating Out section).

They have been making it since the Middle Ages and today the Chaource cheese has the accolade of being one of just 36 French cheeses with an AOC label - Appellation d'Origine Contrôllé and can be found in any one of Champagne's gastronomic joints.

Nevertheless Chaource town also has a lot to offer nature lovers. The Champagne Wetlands "Champagne Humide" have left the landscape of Chaource, located a mere 29km from Troyes, beautifully green and is found in the heart of the Armance forest, almost on the border with Burgundy. The Crogny forest is also nearby.

Architecturally, there are a few 15th century timber-framed houses dotted around but the best monument is to be seen in St-Jean Baptiste church.

Getting There:
Head to Troyes on the following roads: RN17, RN77, A5, A26. It is on the intersection of the D443 and D444

Tourist Information:
Syndicat d'Initiative de Chaource
Route de Troyes à Bruyères
Tel: 00 33 (0)03 25 40 13 45
www.chaource.fr

Tourist Office
Place de l'Eglise
Tel: 00 33 (0)325 40 97 22

Chaource Sights

Eglise Saint-Jean-Baptiste
St-Jean Baptiste Church
Place de L'Eglise

This church, a chorus of Gothic style, has a number of distinctions. The stained glass windows display a mix of local and Italian art, the entombment in the chapel to the left of the 13th century chancel is carved in 1515 by the Master of Chaource and the gilded wooden crib located in the third chapel on the left is believed to be the oldest in France.
Open daily 8.30am-7pm to Oct. & 8.00am- 6pm in winter.
Call in advance for a guided tour.

Musée de Fromage
Cheese Museum
Place de L'Eglise
Tel: 00 33 (0)3 25 40 10 57

This unique museum shows the evolution of cheese making through the ages with a film presentation and displays of various utensils. Though Chaource cheese dominates the film, it also mentions other local cheeses such as Mussy, Ervy and Soumaintrain. The hour long tour ends with a cheese tasting accompanied with a glass of Burgundy wine or cider.

Twice a year in March and October the museum holds a day of heritage, nature and cheese. Visitors can see how beer and cheese is made and learn about the local area and beyond. Tastings of various cheeses are also on the agenda.
Open daily July 1-30 Sep except Tues.
From Oct 1-June 3 open weekends and bank holidays.
Entry: 4 euros.

Musée des Poupées d'Antan et de la Tonnellerie
Antique Dolls Museum
Maisons-lès-Chaource
Located 7 miles south on D34
Tel: 00 33 (0)3 25 70 07 46

The Musée des Poupées d'Antan et de la Tonnellerie is a museum of antique dolls and cooperage. There are some fine examples of porcelain dolls and a reconstruction of a cooper's workshop. The visit ends with a cheese tasting and an aperitif.
Open daily 9am-12pm & 2pm-6pm

Haute Marne

Located at the crossroads of Burgundy and Lorraine is Haute Marne, a stretch of 590,000 acres of lakes, forests, a fortified town and thermal baths

Haut Marne, found South of Champagne, at the crossroads of Burgundy and Lorraine is blessed with 590,000 acres of forests - that equates to almost three acres of forest per inhabitant. Within that landscape, stags stroll freely around the wooded hills, woodland plants flourish and and a lush nature prevails. Streams meander here and there made up by the Aube, Marne, Meuse and Vingeanne rivers all flowing through the entire region. This makes the region a honeypot for water sport lovers and indeed anglers. Trekking is particularly favoured in the east where the landscape is blessed with valleys.

In the north, in **Saint-Dizier** is the largest man-made lake in Europe - the 4,900ha **lac du Der-Chantecoq**. The lake has become a haven for birds and watersport enthusiasts.

The region has more than its fair share of water, and this is exploited in the spa town of **Bourbonne-les-Bains** - a town renowned since the Roman times, for the healing, soothing quality of its water.

Many famous names are connected with the Haut Marne: Charles de Gaulle is buried in **Colombey-les-deux-Eglises** in the northern part of the region; Voltaire escaped imprisonment in the Bastille and fled to **Château de Cirey sur Blaise** where he lived in exile with his mistress Madame de Châtelet.

> **Getting There:**
> From Calais take A26 for 126 miles then N44
>
> **Tourist Information:**
> Haut-Marne Tourist Board
> 40 bis, Avenue Foch
> Chaumont
> t: 00 33 325 87 67 67
> www.tourisme-hautemarne.com

Haute Marne

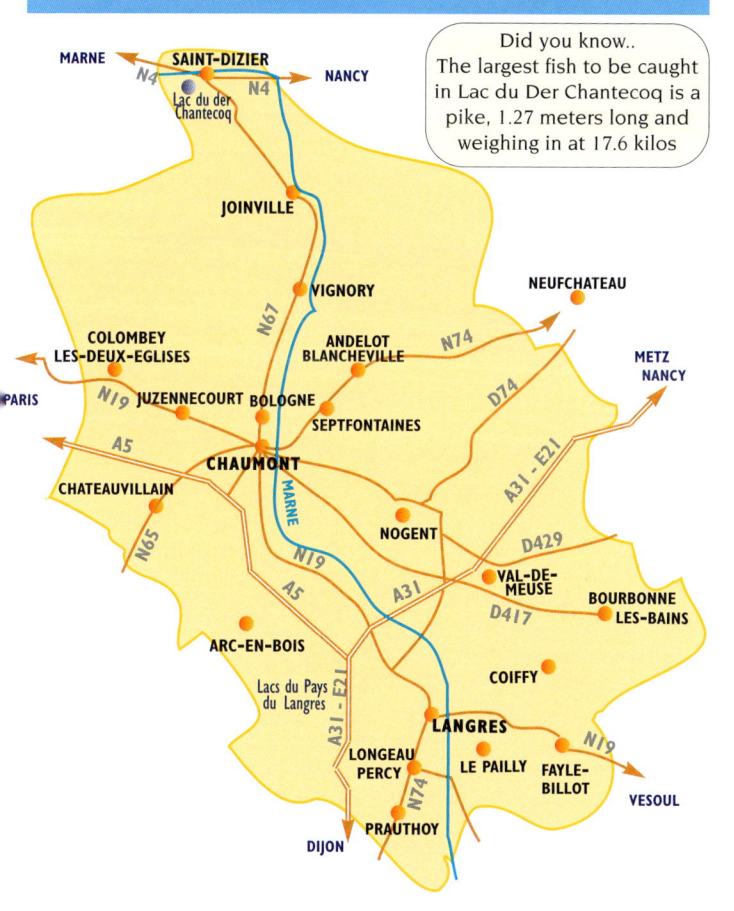

> Did you know..
> The largest fish to be caught in Lac du Der Chantecoq is a pike, 1.27 meters long and weighing in at 17.6 kilos

Haut Marne Must Sees

The Haut Marne has some unusual sights that should not be missed!

Zoo de Bois
Head for **Prez-sous-lafauche** via the **N74** between Chaumont and Neufchâteau and be enchanted. Deep in the forest is a museum of 'found art", the only one in France. It consists of a collection of branches resembling people, scenes, animals that have been placed in amusing places.

Colombey-Les-Deux-Eglises
Take the **N67** to visit this town to see **La Boisserie** where General de Gaulle lived and also the cemetery where he rests. At church he would sit between the stained glass windows of Jeanne d'Arc and Saint Louis.
La Boisserie Tel: 00 33 (0)25 01 52 52

Menhir de La Haute Borne
In Fontaines-sur-Marne, near St Dizier, there is a Megalith which is roughly 4000 years old. It is more than 7m high and when archeologists were excavating in the 19th century it broke into two pieces. It was restored in 1845.

La Cascade d'Etuf
The Petrified Waterfall
East of Langres on the **D20** in **Rouvres** there is a fantastic waterfall tumbling down limestone and through a forest over porous tufa stone. The water from the hillside collects onto a shaded site then separates into smaller but no less splendid falls.

Bourbonne-les-Bains
This **spa** on the **D417** town, famed for its thermal water, specialises in rheumatology, osteoarthritis and respiratory conditions. To find out more contact the tourist office of **Bourbonne-les-Bains, Centre Borvo**, Tel: 00 33 (0)325 90 01 71 www.bourbonne-thermes.fr.

Also in Bourbonne-les-bains is the Bannie Animal Park with a fine aviary and where stags, wild boar and deer roam freely while humans look on. It's open to visitors during the summer and is great for picnics.

Saint Dizier

Saint Dizier is as a modern, industrial town.

Unlike its counterparts of the region Saint Dizier is a modern industrial town where smelting works, ironworks and steelworks have congregated. It was at these ironworks that Hector Guimard, one of the pioneers of Art Nouveau in France chose to make his creations in 1900. Inhabitants commissioned him to decorate their houses both inside and out. You can see his decorative work on the balconies, window sills, palmettes and banisters of the local houses especially in **rue de l'Arquebuse**, **rue du Colonel-Raynal** and **rue du Général-Maistre**. Enthusiasts should get a route map of his works from the tourist office.

Many battles took place here and thus it was used as a stronghold with a garrison of 2,500 soldiers. In 1544 it withstood an attack from the Holy Roman Emperor Charles V and his army of 100,000 men. Napoleon enjoyed his last victory at Saint Dizier before he was exiled to Elba.

The **Quartier de la Noue** suburb was once animated by the work of the boatmen who floated wood logs along the River Marne in flat bottom containers called 'marnois'. They lived in low houses that overlooked gardens and fields. The 80 small alleyways known as 'voyottes', lay at right angles to **avenue de la République** and can still be seen today.

> **Getting There:**
> A26 to Reims, A4 Exit 26: Châlons-Cormontreuil.N44 via Châlons-en-Champagne, N4 via Vitry-le-François to Saint-Dizier.
>
> **Tourist Information:**
> 4 avenue de Belle-Forêt sur Marne
> Tel: 00 33 (0)325 05 31 84

> Did you know...
> that the inhabitants of Saint-Dizier are called the Bragards, a deformation of the term 'braves gars" which means "good sort"

Chaumont

Chaumont has been dubbed 'the Poster Town' because it has a world class collection of posters and graphic art

The medieval town of Chaumont-en-Bassigny, the capital of Haute Marne, is famous for its huge collection of posters. Every year during June the town throws an International Poster and Graphic Arts Festival (Festival International de l'Affiche) attracting visitors from across the globe.

Chaumont is located on the edge of a steep plateau between the River Suize and the River Marne and remnants from its medieval past include the 12th century keep (**Donjon**) of the former feudal castle of Chaumont where the Counts of Champagne resided. These days temporary exhibitions are held here and visitors can enjoy the view over the valley of the River Suize and the town. Along the ramparts is also the hexagonal 13th century **Tour d'Arse**.

It is very pleasant to walk around this town with its pretty houses especially in **Rue Guyard** where there is a fine Renaissance mansion and in **rue Gouthière** where some of the old houses have corbelled turrets with spiral staircases. In the nearby **rue Decrès** look out for the small, overhanging turret and check out number 17 to admire the Louix XIV doorway. To see the highest turret in the town take a look at number 22 **rue St Jean**.

The most famous monument must be the **railway viaduct** built in 1857. You get to it from the D65, considered an elegant piece of 19th century engineering. It stretches some 600m across the Suize Valley at a height of 50m and incorporates 50 three-storey arches, the first being a pedestrian walkway, and the third carries the railway line into the town.

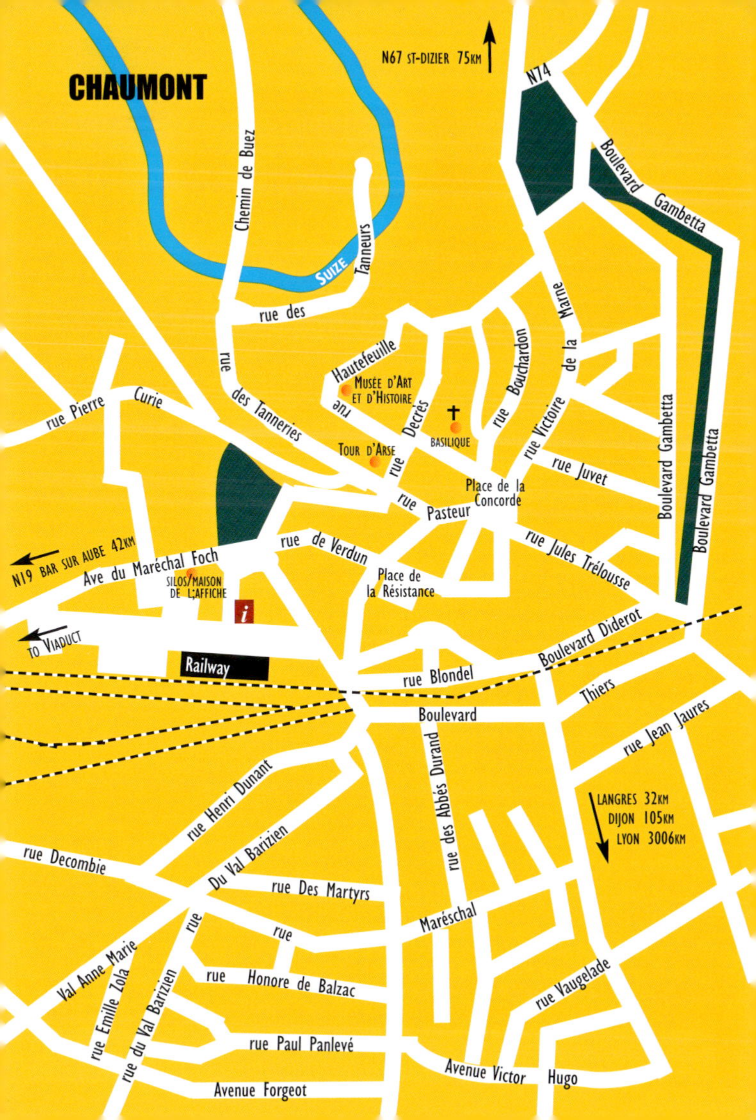
CHAUMONT
N67 ST-DIZIER 75KM
N74
Suize
Chemin de Buez
Tanneurs
rue des
Boulevard Gambetta
rue de la Marne
rue Bouchardon
Hautefeuille
rue
Musée d'Art et d'Histoire
rue des Tanneries
rue Pierre Curie
rue Decrès
Basilique
rue Victoire
rue Juvet
Tour d'Arse
Place de la Concorde
rue Pasteur
Boulevard Gambetta
Boulevard Gambetta
rue de Verdun
rue Jules Trélousse
N19 BAR SUR AUBE 42KM
Ave du Maréchal Foch
Silos/Maison de L;Affiche
Place de la Résistance
i
TO VIADUCT
Railway
Boulevard Diderot
rue Blondel
Thiers
Boulevard
rue Jean Jaures
rue des Abbés Durand
rue Henri Dunant
LANGRES 32KM
DIJON 105KM
LYON 3006KM
rue Decombie
Du Val Barizien
rue Des Martyrs
Maréschal
rue
rue
Val Anne Marie
rue Honore de Balzac
rue Emille Zola
rue du Val Barizien
rue Vaugelade
rue Paul Panlevé
Avenue Victor Hugo
Avenue Forgeot

Chaumont Sights

Basilique St-Jean Baptiste
Probably the most beautiful building in Chaumont is the Basilique St Jean Baptiste. It became a collegiate church in 1474 then a basilique in 1948. The west front dates back to the 13th century and whose gothic transept and east end are 16th century. Everywhere the eye falls is an ornate carving or stonework to admire but the best monument is in the chapel at the west of the nave - an entombment of 1741with eleven life-size statues who seem to evoke a live like expression and attitude. On the exterior around the north side are some interesting flying buttresses and gargoyles.

Musée d'Art et d'Histoire
Place du Palais
Tel: 00 33 (0)325 03 01 99
Located in the vaulted rooms of the former castle of the Counts of Champagne are a variety of paintings from various periods and schools including Flemish, Italian and Spanish, sculptures and archeological artefacts. Included are Fragments of the funeral monument of Antoinette de Bourbon and Claude de Lorraine by Donimique Florentin.
Open daily 2-6pm. Summer 2.30pm-6.30pm
Entry 1.50 euro. Kids and students free.

Les Silos, Maison du livre et de l'affiche
7-9 avenue Foch
Tel: 00 33 (0)325 03 86 86
A former grain silos has been converted into a cultural centre with a library and reference room with multi-media facilities. There is also a poster museum with an impressive 10,000 posters included works by Jules Chéret (1836-1932), Théophile Alexandre Steinlen (1859-1923) and Henri de Toulouse-Lautrec (1864-1901).
Open Tues, Thur, Fri 2pm-7pm. Wed and Sat 10am-6pm. Entry is free.

Musée de la Crèche
rue des Frères-Mistarlet
Tel: 00 33 (0)325 32 39 85
A collection of nativity scenes complete with figurines made of wax are on display dating from 17th-20th centuries. Check out the 18th century crèches from Naples.
Open daily except Tues. 2pm-6pm
Entry : 1.50 euro Kids and students free.

Langres

Not as well known as the other towns of Champagne-Ardenne, but no less quaint or historic.

Langres, known as Andemtunnam in Roman times, in the Haut Marne region of Champagne-Ardenne is not only a walled city, not only an historic monument but also a city that has produced one of the world's greatest philosophers and most importantly produces its very own cheese. All things considered it is amazing that this is the least known of all Champagne's towns.

Perhaps this is because langres is a bit of a no-man's land. Geographically it is located within the bounds of the Haut Marne department of Champagne-Ardenne, an area that does not produce any Champagne and therefore gets overlooked, yet historically it belongs to Burgundy, Burgundy wine being the wine of choice here, but it is not on the Burgundian tourist route.

The approach to Langres gives way to the utterly captivating vision of a dainty walled town perched on a limestone promontory jutting

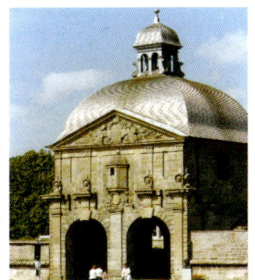

Getting There:
A26 to Reims, A4 Exit 26: Châlons-Cormontreuil.N44 via Châlons-en-Champagne, N4 via Vitry-le-François to Saint-Dizier., N67 then N19

Tourist Information:
Langres Office of Tourism
Square Olivier-Lahalle
52201 Langres
t: 00 33 325 87 67 67
www.tourisme-langres.com

Porte Des Moulins
The gate of Moulins
One of the seven gates. It was protected by the Navarre Tower.

Langres

out between the Bonnell Valley to the west and the Marne Valley to the east. The city is almost surrounded by ramparts with staggering views taking in the man-made lake of Lac de La Liez and the Marne Valley. A walk around the ramparts is easy as there are only 3.5km of walls punctuated with 7 gates and no less than 12 towers.

Ambling around the wall and into the maze of streets is like a live history lesson which encompasses the Gallo-Roman period, ancient monuments and graceful sculptures each tagged with a wall plate with explanations in both French and English.

Some buildings in the cocoon of streets are adorned with statues on the exterior that reflect a fervent popular piety. This is after all a Cathedral town sitting in the shadow of the St-Mammes' Cathedral. It dates back to the 12th century and its impressive 13th century cloister remains in-tact. Like everything else in Langres the

Statue of Diderot, the world famous philosopher and one of Langres' most famous sons.

Cathedral is just a short walk from place Diderot, the main square and the birth place of Diderot the philosopher.

On the surface the city of just 8000 inhabitants looks sleepy and slow paced, but hardly a day passes without some festival or other. It even has its own film festival, its own music and comedy festival as well as a number of historical and thespian festivals where the whole town participates. Unlike Diderot who compiled the 'Encyclopedie' to ensure that information is not lost, today's Langroise simply canonise their heritage in festivity and gastronomy. Glass of Burgundy anyone?

Langres Sights

Cathedrale Saint-Mammes

This huge monument, dating back to 8th century, has ample dimensions measuring 96 metres in length and 23 metres in height. It can accommodate several thousand people at any one time.

Initially the cathedral was dedicated to Saint Jean the Evangelist but was later placed under the patronage of St Mammes.

The cathedral's architecture is a mix of Romanesque and Gothic styles having been started in 1150 and finished in 1196. It is a shining example of how the two 'styles' can complement each other.

Items that must not be missed in the cathedral are the:

- Amoncourt Chapel (1549-51) which has a tiled earthenware glazed floor from Masseot Abaquesne from Rouen and a 14th century Virgin and Child in alabaster.
- The tapestries by Jean Cousin (1544-45)
- Choir gates, panelling and large organ (18th century) from the former Abbey of Mormonod.
- Bas-relief (16th century) which depicts the transfer of the relics of Saint Mammes
- Treasure House.

Legend has it that....

Around 755 a pilgrim carrying a bone from the nape of Saint Mammes's neck returned from Constantinople. He took rest near to Langres hanging his relics in a bag on the branch of a tree with just a thin piece of silk. However he could not retrieve the bag. He went to get help from Bishop Vandier. Accompanied by his clergy and other followers they too could not unhook the bag. At that moment an old man suggested to the bishop that the cathedral be dedicated to Saint Mammes claiming that Saint Jean the Evangelist would not object. The dedication took place and when it was done the relics fell from the tree by themselves. The old man was Saint Jean himself

Langres Sights

Musée d'Art et d'Histoire
Place du Cenenaire
Langres
Tel: 00 33 (0)325 87 08 05
museedelangres@worldonline.fr

Built in the centre of the old town, this architecturally modern museum has fabulous natural lighting thanks to huge expanses of windows. The rest of the building is constructed with concrete, metal and wood making an harmonious if unlikely alliance.

Collections include 17th and 18th century paintings as well as prehistory and early history tools from old excavations. Many Gallo-Roman examples such as a multicoloured mosaic of around 50 metres square representing Bacchus are on show (see image). So are Egyptian exhibits including coins from the Ptolemaic period and scarab amulets.

A gently sloping ramp leads visitors into the church of St Didier, a listed building.

Langres Sights

**Navarre Tower and Orval Tower
Tours Navarre et D'Orval**

The Navarre Tower, 20 metres high and 28 metres in diameter with 20 embrasures spread over four levels, is one of the most imposing of the royal towers and in terms of defence it was also the most prepared.

You will find it on a terrain once owned by the Counts of Champagne a.k.a. Kings of Navarre (hence the name), where its erection commenced in 1512. It looks like an impregnable dungeon, and indeed the walls are seven metres thick in order to protect two vaulted rooms which are powerfully casemated. The cannons on the roof terrace used to protect the 'Moulins' Gate and its entrances.

In the early 19th century le Génie transformed the tower into a gunpower factory. That's when the cone-shaped roof with a frame was bolted on in order to protect the lower levels from leaks. The frame, of chestnut wood, is 29metres in diameter and 12 metres high (see inset).

Two medieval and monstrous gargoyles, appear one higher than the other and apart from grimacing at visitors, mark out where the the roof was raised higher.

Next to the tower is a camp site. Under the ancient Régime the Champ de Navarre (Navarre Field) was home to the 'jeu de l'"Arquebuze'- a shooting competition organised by the Chevaliers de l'Arquebuze for followers of the practice. On the mark of a drum roll participants would take their place and target a metal bird on the end of a stick on top of the Orval tower. The winner would be declared King of the Arquebus.

Avenue de l'Europe
Porte Sous-Murs
Sous-Murs Tower
Allée des Marronniers
Henri IV Gate
Virot Tower
P
Chapel & Dome
Pl. Jean Duvet
St Mammès Cathedral & Cloister
rue de la Charité
rue de la Crémallère
rue du Petit-Cloitre
rue du Grand-Cloitre
Long-Porte
rue Longe-Porte
rue Barbier d'Aucourt
rue Aubert
rue Leclerc
Pl. Diderot
rue de la Clochette
rue de la Croisette
rue Roger
Henriot Square
rue Tassel
rue Defay
rue Boivin
Art & History Museum
Pl. du Centenaire
rue Lambert
Pl. des Jacobins
rue Cardinal Morlot
Pl. Ziégler
rue Richard de Foulons
rue Chambrûlard
rue P Durand
rue Charles Beligné
rue de la Tournelle
rue des Ursulines
rue aux Fées
rue Boulière
rue des Terreaux
Ave de la Colliniere
St-Jean Tower
St Didier Tower
Porte Neu
Petit Sault Tower
Town Hall
Gallo-Roman Gate
Allée du Souvenir Francais
Paris, Reims, Chaumont

Jean Lepetz
RN19
iers
Porte des Auges
rue des Auges
ombard
RN74
Lyon, Dijon
Pl. des Etats-Unis
Ave Turenne
rue Diderot
rot
i
The Mill Gate
P
Parc de Blanchefontaine
Ave Capitaine Baudoin
St Martin Church
rue Minot
Pl. Jenson
Gambetta
rue des Chavannes
rue Mermoz
rue Bezançon
rue 8 Mai 1945
Orval & Navare Towers
LANGRES

Champagne Wine - The History

**According to popular belief, the bubbly nectar was invented by Dom Pérignon.
Not so, but he was a marketing genius.**

Most people will thank **Dom Pérignon** for inventing bubbly Champagne. The 17th century Benedictine monk is generally accredited for putting the bubbles in Champagne, albeit quite inadvertently.

Before Dom Pérignon arrived on the scene, all the wine of Champagne was still wine.

The effervescent 29 year old took his place as 'procureur' at the Abbey of Hautvillliers in the Marne Valley, one of the oldest Benedictine Abbeys in the world. Part of his remit was to sell the wines produced in the surrounding vineyards. But there were problems. When transported on long journeys, the warm weather would result in the wine fermenting in the bottle consequently producing bubbles. For Pérignon and his contemporaries, this was the sign of a bad wine.

He spent many years trying to rid the "mad wine" of these pesky bubbles but he was simply defeated by nature.

Undeterred, he donned his marketing hat and worked hard in creating the perception that bubbly wine was the best thing since... non-sparkling wine and in a short time, sparkling wine caught on.

His genius did not end there. He also developed the art of blending grapes and also blending the juice from the same grape grown in different places. What's more he developed a way to press black grapes to extract white juice, This did wonders for the clarification process creating brighter wine. He used stronger bottles (developed by the English who had been enjoying sparkling wine for some time) to prevent exploding by using Spanish corks instead of wood and oil-soaked hemp stoppers

Champagne Wine - The History

to close the bottles.

Dom Pérignon died in 1715 having spent 47 years of his life as a cellar master at the Abbey of Hautvillliers. In that time he not only developed and formalised the principles of champagne wine making that are still in use today, but he also planted the seeds for an entire industry that would bring immense wealth to the region.

At first it was enjoyed by both the English and French royalty invoking the wine with a sense of prestige. Louis XV took an interest in this popular nectar and in 1728 he allowed wine to be transported in bottles. By 1735 he decreed what that the size, shape and weight of champagne bottles and even the size of the cork should be.

Like any business, expansion and growth involves the hands of more people and soon the monastic and aristocratic growers were replaced with champagne merchants and champagne houses.

They contributed a great deal of capital and talent and expertise into the industry, They strove to improve the wine by stabilising the fermentation process, and of course importantly increasing the distribution of the wine. By 1853 sales of champagne were toppling 20 million bottles.

The industry was stalled by World War I which saw the roman chalk quarries beneath Reims that once stored champagne, being used as shelters while the ground above was bombarded. This was followed by the Russian Revolution and American prohibition. The industry dried up. When prohibition was repealed in 1934, Robert-Jean de Vougë, head of Moët et Chandon managed to set the price of grapes allowing growers to make a good living.

After World War II sales kept on climbing as the different price points have made it more accessible to more people. But the wine has never lost its prestige.

Champagne Wine - The Making

What goes into making this much coveted bubbly?

There are various elements that in concert can bring you a fine flute of fizz.

Firstly you need the right type of earth and a cool climate. In Champagne country the vines struggle to develop and grapes take an age to ripen. When harvested they are rarely ripe enough to make table wine without a lot of sugar additive. So producers make a wine with low alcoholic strength then during the second fermentation the alcohol levels are raised and bubbles develop. The natural high level of acidity inherent in the unripe grapes is great for ageing well in the bottle.

Then you need the right types of grapes. The grapes of Champagne are two-thirds black, chiefly **Pinot Noir** of fine red Burgundy wine fame. Though the skins are black, the juice is white.

The other black grape is **Pinot Meunier**, which makes a softer, fruitier style, important in producing easy drinking wines.

The white grape is **Chardonnay** of white Burgundy fame. This produces a lighter, fresher juice, and the resulting Champagnes are certainly the most perfumed and honeyed. They have been criticised as lacking depth and ageing potential but this is not generally true. Good Blanc de Blanc has a superb, exciting flavour which is only improved by ageing.

The making of champagne wine is a simple but lengthy step by step procedure based on fermentation and gas. It is a cycle that starts by harvesting, by hand the best grapes and can end up to ten years later in a flute.

The process of fermentation converts sugar into alcohol and

Champagne Wine - The Making

carbonic gas supplies the bubbles. The gas is captured in the second fermentation within the confines of a sealed container. When the container is opened the gas produces the tiny, much loved bubbles.

There are two methods of making fizzy wine. The first, **Cuve Close**, produces inferior wine but much cheaper to buy. Other words that describe this process are 'Charmat' or 'tank'. Both the fermentations take place in large vats and are bottled under pressure. Italy's Asti is made this way.

The greatest style of sparkling wine is made in the **Méthode Champenoise**. This is a process where the first fermentation takes place in oak barriques and the second in the actual bottle. Wines produced this way are 'brut' - dry.

First a base wine has to be made - **Cuvée**. Very careful pressing of the grapes in enormous square vertical presses draw off the juice as pale as possible being careful

Champagne is bottled in 10 bottle sizes:
Quarter bottle
– 18.7cl / 6.3 fluid ozs
Half bottle
– 37.5cl / 12.7 fluid ozs
Bottle
– 75cl / 25.4 fluid ozs
Magnum (two bottles)
– 1.5 litres / 50.8 fluid ozs
Jeroboam (four bottles)
– 3 litres / 101.6 fluid ozs
Rehoboam (six bottles)
– 4.5 litres / 147 fluid ozs
Methuselah (eight bottles)
– 6 litres / 196 fluid ozs
Salmanazar (12 bottles)
– 9 litres / 304.8 fluid ozs
Balthazar (16 bottles)
– 12 litres / 406.4 fluid ozs
Nebuchadnezzar (20 bottles)
– 15 litres / 508 fluid ozs

to not allow the colour and bitter qualities from the skins of the black grapes into the juice. Even so, the black grape juice does have a fairly big feel to it, and a Champagne relying largely on black grapes is certain to be heavier and take longer to mature. Yeast is then

Champagne - The Making

added to the juice for the first fermentation. When the first fermentation is complete the juice from the various grape varieties will be blended (known as **assemblage**) according to house style to make the base wine - Cuvée. There may be tens of different base wines blended for use in non-vintage Champagne sometimes reaching up to 80 different wines. Vintage champagne is made only from grapes harvested during a specific year and this only happens when the harvest is exceptional. These are aged longer than non-vintage wines (three years is the minimum for vintage wines whereas non-vintage wines are aged for fifteen months) and are more expensive.

Most Champagne houses put their wines through **Malolactic Conversion**. This is a process that converts hard malic acid into soft lactic acid. The result is a wine with a creamy quality. But some notable houses such as Bollinger, Krug and Lanson choose to prevent this.

After the second fermentation in the bottle courtesy of the yeast, it settles at the bottom and forms a sediment called 'lees'. The yeast has to be removed and this is done by encouraging it to move into a small plastic pot at the neck of the inverted bottled by **riddling (remuage)**. This entails eight weeks of turning the bottles by hand, or eight days by machine. The bottle is then immersed into freezing brine, the cap taken off and the sediment is ejected. All that is left is to fill space left by the disgorgement with a **liqueur d'expédition** - a dosage of liquid sugar.

Voila!

Riddling (remuage) machines used to turn bottles to encourage the yeast to the neck of the bottle.

Champagne Styles

Styles

Each Champagne house will have its own style, their signature if you like. This is acquired through their preferred blend of grapes, or indeed no blend at all.

For instance, a Blanc de Blancs champagne will be made purely from the white popular Chardonnay grape and tend to be delicate, crisper and light-bodied whereas Blanc de Noirs will be softer, medium bodied and creamier.

Champagne Veuve Clicquot, one of the oldest and most distinguished Houses, is known for its full-bodied wines, due to the high proportion of Pinot Noir grapes used in its cuvée or Champagne blend.

The point of the consistency in the blend is to ensure that no matter where in the world you taste a champagne from your favourite house, it will be consistent in quality, body and in taste.

PPOPULAR PRODUCERS AND THEIR BODY

(Body refers to the combination of fruit and alcoholic strength giving an impression of weight in the mouth)

Light Bodied	Medium Bodied	Full Bodied
Laurent-Perrier	Charles Heidsieck	Bollinger
Perrier-Jouët	Deutz	Delamotte
Taittinger	Joseph Perrier	Gosset
	Moët & Chandon	Heidsieck Monopole
	Mumm	Henriot
	Piper-Heidsieck	Krug
	Pol Roger	Louis Roederer
	Pommery	Vueve Clicquot

Champagne Styles

Somewhere in the world a champagne cork pops every 2 seconds. How do you like yours?

Extra Brut, Brut Sauvage, Ultra Brut, Brut Intégral or Brut Zéro
Hardly seen, these are bone dry wines with less than .6% of residual sugar per litre.

Brut
This is the most popular style of champagne. The best blends are always reserved for the brut. It has less than 1.5% residual sugar and is very dry.

Extra Dry, Extra Sec
Sweetened with 1.2 to 2% residual sugar per litre. It is suitably dry to accompany desserts and wedding cakes superbly.

Sec
Although it means "dry" in French, it actually means "moderately dry" or "slightly sweet" when it pertains to champagne. It has 1.7 to 3.5% residual sugar per litre.

Demi-Sec
This style would suite those with a sweet tooth. It contains between 3.3 to 5% residual sugar per litre.

Doux
This is the sweetest style of champagne. It is very sweet and is more of a dessert-style wine. It has a minimum of 5% residual sugar per litre.

Blanc de Noirs
This is made entirely from black grapes but is white. It tends to be fuller than those with Chardonnay in the blend.

Blanc de Blancs
This is made exclusively from Chardonnay grapes and is the most delicate of champagnes. As only 25% of Champagne is planted with Chardonnay, this tends to cost a little more.

> Did you know...
> There are on average 50 million bubbles in a bottle of champagne!

Champagne Labels

What's in a label?
Here are some phrases and codes to help you decipher a label

Grand Cru:
Champagne made from grapes grown on land graded 100% suitable for growing black and white grapes.

Premier Cru:
Champagne made from grapes grown on land graded 90-99% suitable for growing black and white grapes.

RM (Recolant-Manipulant):
Wine made by a grower, not a co-operative or Merchant.

RC (Recolant-Cooperateur):
A grower sells his grapes to a co-operative and buys some wine out of the communal vats to sell under his own name.

CM (Co-operateur-Manipulant):
This is the wine made by and sold by a co-operative.

NM (Negociant-Manipulant):
Wine made and sold by a merchant.

MA (Marque d'Acheteur):
Wine made by a merchant under a second, subsidiary label to satisfy a foreign buyer's wish for a special selection, or to sell at a lower price yet avoid conflict with his chief brand.

SR (Societe de Recoltants):
Wine made by a family company of growers.

Recently Disgorged:
These bottles, usually containing de luxe champagne, have lain on their yeast deposits for much longer than usual, gaining depth and flavour to keeping maximum freshness. The disgorging takes place just before the wine is sold.

> Did you know...
> That only sparkling wine produced in Champagne can include the word 'champagne' on the label.

Champagne Wine Routes

MARNE

Massif de St-Thierry
Vallée de l'Ardre

REIMS ①

Montagne de Reims   Rilly-la-Montagne ② ③ ④ Verzenay
Chigney-les-Roses

Dormans

**CHATILLON-SUR
-MARNE**

⑫ Louvois
Mardeuil ⑯ ⑮ Ay   ⑪ Bouzy   ⑤ Ambonnay

Vallée de la Marne

Château-Thierry   **EPERNAY** ⑭

⑰ Le Breuil   ⑩ Chouilly

⑥

Mareuil-sur-Ay ⑬   ⑨ Avize   **CHALONS-EN
CHAMPAGNE**

Côtes des Blancs

⑦ Mesnil-sur-Oger

SÉZANNE

⑧ Vertus

Pont-St Marie ⑩

TROYES ⑪ Montgueux

**Bar sur
Aube** ①

Ville sur Arce
Grande-au-Rez. ⑨ ⑬   ② Barroville
Buxeuil ⑫   ③ Urville
Celles sur Ource ⑤   ④ Bligny
Polisy ⑥

AUBE

⑦ Gyé sur Seine

Channes ⑧   Les Riceys

102

Champagne Wine Routes

**There are over 12000 Champagne Houses
Here are some of the principle Champagne Houses**

Ambonnay M5
Henri Billiot

Avize M9
Jacques Selosse
Union Champagne

Ay M15
Henri Giraud **V**
Gatinois
Gosset
Gratien
Besserat de Bellefon

Bar-sur-Aube A1
Albert Beerens
Devaux

Bouzy M11
André Clouet

Chigney-les-Roses M3
George Gardet

Chouilly M10
Nicolas Feuillatte
R & L Legras

Epernay M14
A. Charbaut
Alfred Gratien **V**
de Castellane **V**
Besserat de Bellefon
Gratien
Mercier **V**
Perrier-Jouët **V**

Le Breuil M17
Jean Moutardier

Mesnil-sur-Oger M7
Alain Robert
André Jacquart
Delamotte
Launois Père & Fils **V**

Louvois M12
Guy de Chassey

Mardeuil M16
Beaumont des Crayères

Mareuil-sur-Ay M13
Abel Lepitre
Billecart-Salmon
Philipponnat

Montagne de Reims M8
Mailly Grand Cru **V**

Reims M1
Alain Thiénot
Bruno Paillard
Delbeck
Jacquart
Palmer & Co
Pommery **V**
Ruinart **V**
Veuve Clicquot-Ponsardin **V**

Rilly-la-Montagne M2
Canard-Duchêne **V**
Daniel Dumont
Vilmart

Urville A3
Drappier **V**

Vertus M8
Larmandier-Bernier
Napoléon

Verzenay M4
Michel Arnould

V = Accepts visitors   M = Marne   A = Aube

Champagne Wine Routes

Champagne's Sacred Triangle

Champagne's vineyards are located in a clearly defined area whose boundaries were legally set in 1927 and spread out over three of the four departments : Aube and Haute-Marne but most prolific in the Marne. The vineyards are owned by thousands of growers, many of whom work part-time, to supply the grapes for the champagne houses.

However, the most famous route is the **Route du Champagne** which lies within a triangular (very roughly speaking) area formed by **Reims**, **Châlons-sur-Marne** and **Épernay** and is known affectionately as **Champagne's Sacred Triangle**.

The route rambles through the vineyards of the **Montagne de Reims** (where Pinot Noir is mainly planted) the east facing **Côte des Blancs** around 13 miles south of Epernay (where the Chardonnay grape is mainly grown), and the **Marne Valley** (where pinot meunier is grown) eventually wending its way through vineyards and cereal plains reaching out to the densely forested and hilly lake district of the Ardennes in the north. Hautvillers, is located just within the triangle.

The Montagne de Reims portion of this marked route extends from Reims to Épernay and is approximately 47 miles long.

The route is clearly marked with signposts indicating the Champagne towns, the main sites and the small wine villages along the way.

There are no fewer than 2,700 producers and vintners in

Champagne Wine Routes

24 Members of the Club des Grandes Marques

Ayala • Ay
Billecart-Salmon • Mareuil-sur-Ay
Bollinger • Ay **V**
Canard-Duchêne • Ludes
Deutz & Geldermann • Ay
Heidsieck & Co. Monopole • Reims
Charles Heidsieck • Reims
Henriot • Reims
Krug • Reims
Lanson Père et Files • Reims **V**
Laurent-Perrier • Tours-sur-Marne
Moët et Chandon • Epernay **V**
G. H. Mumm • Reims
Perrier-Jouët • Epernay
Joseph Perrier • Châlons-sur-Marne
Piper-Heidsieck • Reims
Pol Roger • Epernay
Pommery & Greno • Reims
Ch. & A Prieur •
Loius Roederer • Reims
Ruinart • Reims
A Salon • Le Mesnil-sur-Oger
Taittinger • Reims
Veuve Clicquot-Ponsardin • Reims **V**

V = Accepts visitors

Champagne, who grow grapes, make wine and, increasingly, sell it using their own names. That's an astonishingly high number, especially considering all the time and money and expertise it takes to make sparkling wine. Many can be visited and some even offer tastings for free.

The biggest and most famous houses are known as **Grandes Marques** or literally big brands.

In 1882, three of the major Champagne houses formed the **Syndicat des Grandes Marques**. Within a year 19 other houses joined it and as a result it represented nearly the whole champagne trade at the time.

By 1993 it was renamed the **Club des Grandes Marques** and was reorganised to include members who adhere to certain minimum quality standards. Currently there are 24 members.

What they all have in common is the classification system. For instance their Grand Cru Champagnes will be made with the grapes (either from their own vineyards or

Champagne Wine Routes

bought in) grown on the 17 finest Grand Cru villages who have been graded to be 100% suitable for producing black and white grapes. Premier Cru wines will have been produced from grapes grown on land graded 90-99 percent suitable from the 38 Premier Cru Villages. Lesser percentage grading are less desirable.

Though not part of the exclusive Club de Grandes Marques, there is also an established group of 'Principal Champagne Houses' among the 12,000 or so dotted around the region. These include famous names such as Mercier, Ruinart and Drappier who are capable of producing prestigious wines.

WINE ROUTES - MARNE

Route 1 (70km)
The Saint Thierry Massif, Ardre Valley

The route starts at Reims and ends at Epernay. It leads you through vineyards and dense forests of the Massif de Saint-Thierry. The region is closely linked to the history of Reims and the coronation of kings ever since Christmas Eve of 496 when Clovis made a gift of the Saint Thierry Massif to Saint Rémi in appreciation of his baptism. Starting at Reims cathedral where 30 kings have been crowned the route then heads north-west towards Tinqueux, Champigny and Merfy where the first sightings of vineyards appear. The village of Saint Thierry was built around the monastery in the year 500 by Saint Thierry. It was destroyed on the eve of the French Revolution in 1789 but the 12th century chapel and ancient chapter room still survive. On the route you pass Savigny-sur-Ardes where Charles de Gaulle made his first radio appeal on 28 May 1940 for the resistance.

Route 2 (70km)
The Montagne de Reims
The National Park

Start at either Reims or Epernay for a trip through the finest wine growing areas of France. The route is signposted in both directions taking you through the 'Champagne and Mystery' trail leading you through Verzy with its 1000 twisted ancient beach trees. This is the highest point on the Montagne de Reims - Mont Sinai (283m). The Vine Museum located in the lighthouse of Verzenay is worth a visit. You can enjoy great views of the vineyards and villages such as Bouzy and Dizy. The Burgomasters' guild at Bouzy has

Champagne Wine Routes

created a 'chemin des vignes', an original guided route that takes you past numerous winegrowers.

Route 3 (90km)
The Marne Valley, The Hills around Epernay
This tour starts and ends at Epernay. Take the right bank along the river Marne and return along the left bank. Ramblers should take the Paradise Path through the vineyards above Epernay. At the first village Chapmillion, stop and stare at the panoramic views over Epernay. Follow the winding path to Hautevilliers to visit the abbey of Dom Pérignon - you have to book your visit in advance with the owners Moët et Chandon. when you get to Oeuilly you may feel the village still lives in the 19th century, especially if you visit the open air museum of Maison Champenoise where the lives of 18th and 19th century winegrowers is depicted.

Route 4 (120km)
The Marne Valley, The Land of La Fontaine
This serene region gave birth to La Fontaine's fables. Start at Château-Thierry. birthplace of Jean de la Fontaine, the 17th century Aesop, passing unspoiled villages, wine cellars and the American Monument of Cote 2004 which commemorates American troops who fought in World War 1.

Route 5 (100km)
Côte des Blancs, Coteaux du Sézannais
Start at the famous Avenue de Champagne in Epernay (home to the most famous champagne houses) and continue north-south through the home of the Chardonnay grape towards Vertus. Pass historical byways and the Sézannais hills and vineyards.

WINE ROUTES - AUBE

Route 1 (240km)
Côte des Bar
Though most wine routes are in the Marne, the Aube too has something to offer. The Côte des Bar has its fair share of vineyards and forests. It is also the region where Renoir spent much of his time. His studio in Essoyes is open to the public. The trail will lead you to Les Riceys, a lovely village of narrow streets and riverside walks. There are three 'Appellations d'Origine Contrôlée' here, the most famous being 'Rosé des Riceys' revered for its bouquet of violets. The route leads southwards to the forest of Clairvaux, where the famous Cistercian abbey founded by Saint Bernard in 1115 is located. Nearby is the 'Cristalleries Royales de Champagne.

Champagne More Than a Quaff?

**Champagne, it is said, is more than just a delicious alchoholic drink.
Some insist it's also a great tonic for many medical conditions**

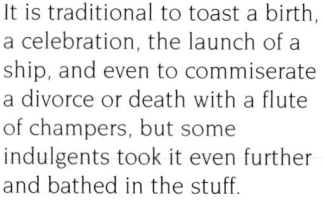

It is traditional to toast a birth, a celebration, the launch of a ship, and even to commiserate a divorce or death with a flute of champers, but some indulgents took it even further and bathed in the stuff.

But amazingly, there are also claims that Champagne is great for certain ailments. The high magnesium and sulphur content is said to help combat a series of food allergies. Some proponents believe it alleviates wind. Proust, for example, drank it to successfully alleviate his abdominal wind and Bismarck, notorious for his flatulence, solved his problem by regularly ingesting this bubbly alternative medicine.

The French believe it alleviates their 'crise de foie' a condition which describes feeling done-in after a bout of over indulgence, others claim it helps with obesity and anxiety, sleeplessness and even migraine. The phrase "I drink to forget" may prove that point.

Many enthusiasts also vouch for the nectar's role as an aphrodisiac especially when taken with chocolate.

This perhaps goes a little way to explaining the active extra-marital exertions the Europeans are so famous for.

Champagne Houses

Can you really visit Champagne wihout visiting a champagne house?

Visiting a champagne house can be a magical experience: the immense cellars, the beautiful chateau and the unfolding story of the complexities involved in making champagne are simply awesome. Luckily many houses open their doors to visits. Some charge a fee but this is worth it for the tour of the cellars that were carved out of chalk many centuries ago (crayeres); the staggering view of tens of thousands of bottles stacked up against the cellar walls at various levels of the production process. That in itself is enough to bring on a raging thirst in time for the tasting that follows. You may also notice elaborate bas-reliefs carved into the chalk face in some cellars, and some may be so big that the tour is taken in an electric car.

Unless you are visiting in September or October, you will not be able to see the harvest (vendage) and the presses (pressoirs) and even then those that do allow this are few. One house that does is Launois in Mesnil sur Oger and they have made the visit into an amazing event.

During a visit you may see giant stainless steel storage tanks where the grape juice (referred to as 'must') is kept until required for blending. You will also be shown the art of riddling (remuage) and disgorgement (degorgement) which are an intrinsic part of making wine in the Methode Champenoise.

Generally you need to make an appointment (rendez-vous) and perhaps arrange a tasting (dégustation). There's no need to feel obliged to buy anything especially if you have paid for the tour and tasting but who knows, you may feel like celebrating and champagne is certainly perfect.

Champagne Houses

Bartnicki Père et Fils Aube 7
22 Grand Rue
Gyé-sur-Seine
Tel: 00 33 (0)325 38 24 53
champagne-bartnickiWwanadoo.fr
www.bartnicki-robin.com
Visits by appointment only. After a tasting in the XVII vaulted cellars, Vincent Bartnicki will show you around the vineyard.

This is a small champagne house with 6 hectares of vineyards. It is located within a charming Champenois village full of stone-built houses surrounded by beautiful landscape. The house has the accolade of being on the picturesque Champagne Touristic Route.

Bartnicki produces four champagnes including a rosé and a vintage champagne made up of 70% Pinot Noir and 30% Chardonnay.

Beaumont de Crayères Marne 16
64 rue de la Liberté
Epernay
Tel: 00 33 (0)326 55 29 40
info@champagne-beaumont.com
www.champagne-beaumont.com
Visits by appointment only. The tour lasts around 40 minutes. Tastings can include all of their eight vintages.
Open: 10am-12pm & 2pm-6pm
Cost: 4 euros

This is a small co-operative in Mardeuil just a hop and skip west of Epernay. They are famous for producing excellent champagnes, many gold medal winners, yet at less than you would expect to pay for such quality. The success of this house is partly due to the fact that this team of 240 independent growers tends to be weekend hobbyists who care for their vineyard (80 hectares in total) with the loving care of any enthusiastic gardener. Visitors to their reception room are greeted by the largest bottle of champagne in the world - it contains 205 bottles of rosé wine equivalent to 195 litres.

The director is the award winning champagne-maker, Jean-Paul Berthus who has taken the house from success to success. Most of their wine- around 80% of its 600,000 bottles - is exported to fifteen countries including Japan.

Champagne Houses

Bollinger Marne 15

16 rue Jules Lobet
Ay-Champagne
Tel: 00 33 (0)326 53 33 66
contact@champagne-bollinger.fr
www.champagne-bollinger.fr
Visits by appointment only. Call for more information. Closed at weekends and bank holidays.

Jacques Bollinger started his career by selling wines for Muller-Ruinart (now known as Henri Abelé) in 1822. He spent seven years there before starting his own company with Paul Renaudin in 1829. They named their house Renaudin Bollinger but this changed in 1984 to Bollinger. The house is still 100% family owned and since the beginning they have been both growers and producers of champagne and owners of 70% of their vineyard sources.

The vintage champagnes are 100% barrel-fermented but their most popular wine the Bollinger Special Cuvée Brut is 50% barrel fermented. Perhaps this is an example of where tradition sells, albeit with a little help from Mr. Bond.

James Bond pledged his loyalty to Bollinger in 1953 when Ian Fleming first penned his first James Bond. In return, the Bond theme is played on Bollinger's answering machine.

Prince Charles counts Bolly as his favourite tipple as does Joanna Lumley aka Patsy in Absolutely Fabulous.

> "I drink it when I'm happy and when I'm sad. Sometimes I drink it when I'm alone. When I have company I consider it obligatory. I trifle with it when I'm not hungry and drink it when I am. Otherwise I never touch it - unless I'm thirsty of course"
> **Lily Bollinger talking about her champagne drinking habits.**

Canard Duchêne Marne 2

1 rye Edmond Canard
Ludes le Coquet, Rilly-La Montagne
Tel: 00 33 (0)326 61 11 60
visite@canard-duchene.fr
www.canard-duchene.fr
**Visits by appointment only. Includes the cellars and a glass of Champagne. You can also visit the art gallery. Closed Sun. and bank holidays.
Cost: 6 euros**

Champagne Houses

<u>Getting</u> <u>There:</u> From Reims Cathedral take A4 towards Metz, exit Conrmontreuil. At 2nd roundabout turn left towards Louvois (D9) for 8km. Ludes is then indicated.

Canard Duchêne is the only champagne house to be located in the heart of the beautiful landscape of Montagne de Reims and have been in Ludes since 1869.

Their fruity flavoured champagnes are reasonably priced and are ideally suited for those easy drinking moments.

Theirs is a love story between Victor Canard and Léonie Duchêne the daughter of winemakers in Ludes. They combined resources to create their own champagne house.

It was their son Edward who put the house on the map by supplying the Court of Tsar Nicolas 2nd. All their labels still carry the two-headed eagle, the emblem of the Russian Imperial family. The third generation of the family in the shape of Victor Canard brought Canard Duchene to the masses by associating with major sports events like the 1968 Winter Olympics in Grenoble.

In 1978 the house was taken over by Veuve Cliquot and was integrated in the LVMH group. In October 2003 it was taken over again by the champagne group Alain Thiénot.

De Castellane Marne 14

57 rue de Verdun
Epernay
Tel: 00 (0)33 326 51 19 11
visites@castellaine.com
www.castellane.com

Open daily 10.00-11.15am & 2-5.15pm
Tours last around 45 minutes and are available in English. The tour includes a visit to their cellars, and the museum and ends with a tasting. On weekdays visitors can view the production lines at work

De Castellane carries the name of one of the oldest families in France dating back to the 10th century during the time of the Counts of Arles and of Provence.

It was in 1895 when Viscount Florens De Castellane founded

Champagne Houses

his Champagne house in Epernay choosing the red Cross of Saint-André as his emblem in honour of the ancient regiment of Champagne.

It is now part of the Laurent-Perrier group but the wines produced by this house tend to be underrated and fabulous value.

De Castellane choose grapes which come from the best vineyards of the Montagne de Reims, the Marne Valley, Côte des Blancs and the Aube district.

A tour to de Castellane will involve an in-depth educational about the champagne making process right through to bottling and labelling.

You will also get to see the fine collection of antique riddling machinery which some may find interesting. Ask to climb their tower, because from here you will gain a panoramic vista over Epernay and the Marne Valley and get to visit their champagne museum.

Château de Bligny Aube 4

10 200 Bligny
Tel: 00 33 (0)325 27 40 11
Open daily 10am-7pm except Sundays and bank holidays. The tour includes a film showing the work involved in making champagne and is followed by a tasting of three wines.
Cost 3 euros. English spoken

Only two champagne houses use the title Château, one of which is Château de Bligny. This magnificent 18th century castle is surrounded with 10ha of parklands full of ancient trees over 100 years old. There is even a sequoia tree of more than 200 years. Built by the Marquis de Dampierre, this castle has been entirely renovated and offers artworks and paintings.

The castle also has a billiards room, a ballroom and a room with over 1000 19th century champagne flutes on display.

Champagne Houses

Drappier Aube 3

Grand Rue
Urville
Tel: 00 33 (0)325 27 40 15
www.champagne-drappier.com
infos@champagne-drappier.com

Open daily except Sundays and bank holidays. Simply turn up if you just want a tasting, but book in advance for a tour of the cellar. Tours last around 45 minutes and are available in English. The tour includes a visit to their cellars and ends with a tasting.

Drappier was established in 1908 in Urville in the heart of the Côte des Bars region, Drappier champagnes have graced the cellars of Charles de Gaulle located in the next village of Colombey Deux Eglises.

Their well-exposed vineyards were planted centuries ago by the Gallo Romans in 1AD on a terroir of high chalk content in the soil. They were further developed by the cistercians of the Clairvaux Abbey. Their 12th century cellars were actually built with the help of Saint Bernard.

The Drappier style is accomplished by a particularly slow fermentation, and the vintage wines mature for many years in the cool darkness of the cellars. After disgorgement, the dosage they top the wine up with is made to a secret family formula that has been aged in oak and glass demijohns.

Their repertoire of fine champagnes include the 'Cart D'Or' Brut made 90% Pinot Noir grapes touched with 5% Meunier and 5% Chardonnay, The Carte Blance Brut, a fresh, fruity yet elegantly light cuvée and their delicious signature wine (each bottle is signed 'Drappier') Blanc de Blanc is composed of 100% Chardonnay

MichelleDrappier in his cellar

Champagne Houses

François Brossolette Aube 6

42 Grand Rue
Polisy
Tel: 00 33 (0)325 38 57 17
françois-brossolette@wanadoo.fr
Visits, tours and tastings are free but by appointment only.
Open daily except Sun.

This twelve-acre champagne house is a relatively young house which combines traditional methods of champagne production with state of the art technology to create their champagnes.

For example they still turn the bottles by hand but use electronic wine-presses and temperature-controlled vats. François Brossolette has achieved the coveted title of "Grand Bouteiller" from the Brotherhood of the "Saulte Bouchon champenois".

G de Barfontarc Aube 2

route de Bar-sur-Aube
Baroville
Tel: 00 33 (0)325 27 07 09
g.de.barfontarc@wanadoo.fr
Open daily 9am-12pm & 1.30pm-5.30pm except Sun. and bank holidays. Narrated tours end with a tasting of 3 champagnes
Visits last around two hours and are by appointment only. English spoken.
Cost 3 euros.

You will find this house on the right hand side as you leave the village. This is a syndicate of winegrowers stretching over 100ha and within that, three villages are represented: Baroville, Fontaine and Arconville.

A tour includes a detailed explanation of how champagne is made and a history of their syndicate.

G de Barfontarc are a member of the "Winegrower's Lunches" programme, "Wine Appreciation" and "Grape Picking" programmes, so feel free to ask about how to participate. Discovery Day Lunches cost around 65 euros and include the meal, visits to associates and various champagne tastings including cuvée Extra quality brut, la cuvée Exception, la cuvée Sainte-Germaine amongst others.

Champagne Houses

Henri Giraud Marne 15
71 Boulevard Charles de Gaulle
Aÿ
Tel: 0 33 (0)3 26 55 18 55
champagne.henri.giraud@wanadoo.fr
www.champagne-giraud.com

Open at weekends by appointment only. Themed visits: how to make champagne Henri Giraud style followed by a tasting of different cuvées.

Henri Giraud Champagne house has been rooted in Aÿ since the 17th century making it the oldest champagne house still owned and run by the same family. Yet it remains one of the smaller 'grand marques' houses of Champagne with all twelve generations selling their wares to a selected clientele.

The house was founded by Francois Hémart who settled in Aÿ in 1625 during the reign of King Louis XIII. In the early 20th century Léon Giraud, a soldier, married into the family and managed to revitalise an ailing vineyard struck down by phylloxera, a disease that can kills vines.

Aÿ has always been regarded as the finest region for champagne production and all of Henri Giraud's wines are Grand Cru wines using only the regulatory Pinor Noir and Chardonnay grapes.

Where stainless steel barrels were becoming popular Henri Giraud still used small oak barrels endowing their wines with fatness and structure. And now for the first time in twenty five years, the wines of Aÿ are being aged as they were by Dom Perignon: in the unique oak barrels of the Argonne Forest, thanks to Claude Giraud. He has had ten 228 litre Argonne oak barrels made especially for him and this decision has borne the house much adulation and lots of medals. Look out for his 2000 vintage in 2007.

Even the bottles used by Henri Giraud are unique, shaped in the form of the ancient "pomponne" glass. The wine information is actually engraved into the glass.

Champagne Houses

Jacky Therrey Aube 9
8 route de Montgueux
La Grande-au-Rez
Tel: 00 33 (0)325 70 30 87
Open daily. Visits and tastings by appointment only.
A small, but nevertheless, award-winning 5.5 acre champagne house. They produce around 25,000 bottles a year. In 2002 their 100% Pinot Noir Rosé champagne won a silver medal in a contest in Epernay. You can buy this tasty number for 12.50 euros.

Jean Velut Aube 10
9 rue du Moulin
Pont-Sainte-Marie
Tel: 00 33 (0)325 74 83 31
Open daily. Visits and tastings by appointment only.
A young, intimate 7ha champagne house established in the 1960's when their village was extended to Montgueux. Jean personally attends to his vnes. They produce a great dry champagne made of 80% chardonnay and 20% pinot noir for just 10,80 euros. Tours are led by a member of the family

Lanson Marne 1
12 boulevard Lundy
51100 Reims
Tel: 00 33 (0)326 78 50 50
**Open Mon-Fri excluding bank holidays, and August.
8.30-11.00 & 14.00-16.30
Tours are in English, French and German and include a visit to their cellar and tasting. Lasts 1 hour.
Cost: 5 euros**

Lanson Champagne house was founded in 1760 making this one of the oldest houses. Back then it was called Delammote after the founder Françoise Delammote who was a Knight of the Order of Malta. The Maltese Cross has always been used as the House crest.

When Delammote died the firm was renamed Veuve Delamotte-Barrachin. His son-in-law Jean Baptiste Lanson was brought into the fold and when Delamotte's widow died in 1837 the name was changed again to Lanson Père & Fils.

In 1980 the Gardinier Group took control of Lanson following the purchase of shares held by Ricard. The company changed hands in

Champagne Houses

1983 to the BSN group and then LVMH in 1990. Four months later Marne et Champagne bought the company.

There are four classic Lanson cuvees and these are the Ivory Label, Rose Label and Gold Label. The Lanson black Label Brut Non vintage is probably the most famous champagne outside of France. It's racy taste and lingering flavours make this an easy drinking, any time anywhere sort of wine.

Each label has its own distinct characteristics brought about by the different grape ratios but they all share a certain freshness. This is due to the decision not to use malolactic fermentation. They are one of the few not to use this process and it certainly works for them.

Launois Père et Fils Marne 7
2 Avenue Eugène Guillaume
51190 Le Mesnil-Sur-Oger
Tel: 00 33 (0)03 26 57 50 15
info@champagne-launois.fr
www.champagne-launois.fr

**Open daily 10.00-11.15am & 2-5.15pm except bank holidays. Tours are available by appointment only. They last around 2 hours and are available in English. The tour includes a visit to their cellars, the museum and ends with a tasting in the cellars.
Cost: 6 euros.
Day programmes involving breakfast, grape picking, tour and lunch cost 58 euros.**

Founded in 1872 this father and son team - Bernard et Dany Launois - run Launois champagne house carrying on the tradition of seven generations. They use the finest grapes to produce la cuvée Réservée, a champagne of 100% Chardonnay grand cru, the champagne Oeil of 100% Pinot Noir, and the slightly sweeter la Cuvée Clémence.

The house is located in the small village of Le Mesnil Sur Oger right in the heart of of the Côtes des Blancs within large wooded grounds. The

Champagne Houses

Renaissance style chateau actually sits within a mini vineyard where the traditional grapes of Champagne grow and all around are droves of doves, swans and ducks.

Over the years, Bernard Launois has managed to assemble a magnificent collection of wine antiques and champagne memorabilia for his museum of the vine and the tour of the chateau and the cellars includes a worthy visit to this museum.

They also run programmes during mid-September to mid-october, where visitors can participate in the harvesting of grapes while enjoying a great deal of gastronomic hospitality.

The program starts a 9am with breakfast at the grape press-house, followed by a trip to the vineyard to participate in grape picking. Later you return to the press for a tasting of the juice, followed by a trip to the museum and then a champagne lunch. The cost is around 58 euros.

Marcel Vérzien Aube 5

68 Grande Rue
Celles-sur-Ource
Tel: 0 33 (0)3 25 38 50 22
contact@champagne-vezien.com
www.champagne-vezien.com

Open Mon. to Sat. from 9am-12 noon & 2pm-6pm but an appointment is required for a tour.
Open by appointment on Sun.
English spoken.

This family owned champagne house was founded by Armand Vézien and sons at the end of the 19th century and the same family - four generations later - continue the champagne production tradition.

There are eight products in their range including the celebrated regional wine Rosé des Riceys.

Tours are conducted by Jean-Pierre who is a member of the "Wine Appreciation" and "Grape-picking" programmes. He is also a Grand Master within the Brotherhood of the "Saulte Bouchon Champenois.

Champagne Houses

Mercier Marne 16

68-70 avenue de Champagne
Epernay
Tel: 00 33 (0)326 51 22 22
www.champagnemercier.com
**Open daily. Closed 11.30-2pm.
Tours, available in English, last around 45 minutes. They include a laser-guided train, the opportunity to view the 160,000 litre barrel that took 20 years to build.
Cost: 6 euros**

Mercier is the brand leader across the channel and certainly France's most popular champagne. Their style tends to be fuller and riper but perhaps less elegant when compared to Moët et Chandon, but they do produce some dazzling fizz.

Touring this house is easy as you do not need to make an appointment. Just turn up during office hours and pay the fee.

The visitor centre is built around the world biggest barrel constructed in 1889. Here you will catch a film and then a lift takes you down 30m into the cellars. The laser-guided train makes its way long the 18km galleries which were once used for car rallies.

The house was founded by the forward thinking Eugène Mercier in 1858. He started by drilling around thirty galleries to be used as cellars and built them on the only bank with access to the railway lines in 1870. The cellars are still fantastic, decorated with reliefs and sculptures.

Their estate extends to 23 ha and represents 25% of their grape production. The rest is bought in.

Mercier Brut is a blend of three grape varieties and a large proportion of Pinot Noir. the Brut Rosé is a mix of Pinot Noir and Meunier.

The 1997 harvest produced a vintage champagne. If you wish to have a multiple tasting, you can do so for a fee of 10 euros which includes the tour and three quality champagnes. Higher fees of between 13 to 43 euros allow for tastings of escalating levels of generosity and quality.

Champagne Houses

Michel Furdyna Aube 5
3 rue Trot, Celles-sur-Ource
Tel: 0 33 (0)3 25 38 54 20
www.champagne-furdyna.fr..fm.
Open Mon. to Sat. from 9am-12 noon & 2pm-6pm. Tours and tastings by appointment only.
Cost: 3,05 euros.

A tour through Michel Furdyna cellars is accompanied by his amusing stories of the surrounding village. Both his Carte Blanche and Demi Sec wines are made with 80% pinot noir and 20% chardonnay. The Réserve is a Blanc de Noirs made from 100% pinot noir. The Rosé is also 100% pinot noir but undergoes a short maceration process.

Michel Leroy-Galland Aube 11
3 m La Grange au Rez
Montgueux
Tel: 0 33 (0)3 25 70 32 91
Open Mon. to Sat. from 9am-12 noon & 2pm-6pm. Tours and tastings by appointment only.

Champagnes are made from grapes harvested from vines of over 25 years old. Michel's tours are lively and enthusiastic.

Moët et Chandon Marne 16
18 avenue de Champagne
Epernay
Tel: 00 33 (0)326 51 20 20
www.moet.com
Open daily 9.30-11.00 am and 2-4.40pm. The cellars of Moët et Chandon are adorned with carefully stacked bottles of Champagne including the staircase and cellars. They span around 17 miles underground.
Tours last around 45-60 minutes some in English and tasting are also available.
Cost: 7.50 euros

During the run up to the Millennium, fake Champagne was being marketed as the real thing - the name on the bottles was Moët et Chandon. Though not desirable this does show the extent of the mass appeal of this famous house.

It was founded in 1743 by a wine trader called Claude Moet, whose ancestors had been in Champagne for generations dating back to the 14th century.

The house really expanded when Jean-Rémy Moet, took over in the 19th century. He had both the friendship and the

Champagne Houses

patronage of Napoleon, who would buy thousands of bottles on his way to battle - except Waterloo and look what happened there.

Jean-Rémy Moet had a keen marketing vision to drive the house to great fame. In 1832 he in turn handed the house to his son and son-in-law Pierre-Gabrel Chandon de Briailles hence the name.

Later on the house had associations with the historical figure Dom Pérignon the 17th century Benedictin monk who is credited with the marketing of Champagne.

Moet bought the Abbey in 1823 and the name from Mercier in 1930, and continued to peddle the legend, placed his statue at the entrance and created the very first prestige cuvée using Dom Pérignon's name. In 1936 their 1921 vintage was launched and they returned to Mercier to buy the entire company. It was since taken over by Louise Vuitton Moet Hennessy group.

Moutard-Diligent Aube 12

rue des Ponts
Buxeuil
Tel: 00 33 (0)325 38 50 73
champagne.moutard@wanadoo.fr
www.champagne-moutard.fr
Open 9am-12pm and 2pm-7pm except Sun. and bank holidays. They also have an annual Open Day on 4th November.

Their vineyard, located on the slopes of the Côte des Bar, dates back to Gallo-Roman times and this family has been making champagne here for several generations since 1642.

At the close of the 19th century, Hyacinthe Diligent was experimenting with techniques for distilling their particular style of champagne. The style she settled on has made their house famous. The same recipe is still used today and has resulted in gold medals.

They also produce other products among them ratafia (a blend of champagne and wine brandy) which recently won a bronze medal in a Paris competition.

Champagne Houses

Mumm Marne 1

34 rue du Champ de Mars
Reims
Tel: 00 33 (0)326 49 59 70
**Tours, available in English, last around 45 minutes plus a video show and a look at ancient vinting tools.
There is a gift shop**
Cost: 5 euros

The Mumm brothers, Jacobus, Gottlieb and Phillipp were from a rich family of German wine merchants. They owned vineyards in the Rhine Valley and expanded to Reims in 1827.

Somehow, Mumm Cordon Rouge has maintained consistent world class quality throughout the centuries. This house is a major player with a standing of being the third largest brand in the world with a yearly production of over 8 million bottles. Thanks to its advances in viticulture and high profile initiative this house has been largely the driving force in the outstanding success of champagne in general around the world. Their wines are characterised by a complex fresh fruit with caramel flavours with a touch of acidity and long length.

Mumm's champagne has been chosen as the official drink of the Formula One Podium

The house is now owned by Allied Domecq spirits and wine.

Pierre Brigandat Aube 8

4 Grande Rue
Channes
Tel: 00 33 (0)325 29 33 49
Visits by appointment only.

The charming village of Channes borders Burgundy and is full of pretty lanes and wonderful stone buildings. Among these is this small family champagne house. They produce some 35,000 bottles every year including the Tradition, Le Prestige and the famous Rosé des Riceys. The range starts with the brut at 10,52 euros. Visitors can taste their champagnes within a charming environment.

Champagne Houses

Perrier Jouet Marne 16

26 avenue de Champagne
51201 Epernay
Tel: 00 33 (0)326 84 43 44
**Open Mon-Fri - not bank holidays
9.00-11.00 & 14.00-16.15
Tours are in English, French and German and include a visit to their caves, the museum and tasting of 3 Champagnes
Cost: on application**
Getting there: via A4 motorway.

The Perrier Jouet story starts with a wedding that took place almost 200 years ago. In 1811, Pierre-Nicolas-Marie Perrier, a cork manufacturer, married Adèle Jouet and set up the champagne trading house Perrier-Jouet, in Epernay. They were amongst the first to use only Chardonnay grapes in their vintage wines endowing the wines with elegance and refinement.

Charles Perrier took over from his father and his house became the first to create a "dry" champagne in 1854 known as "Brut Champagne". They were also one of the first to produce "millésimés" - vintage champagnes. and also the first Champagne house to state the "cru" - village name and the year of the harvest on the cork and by the 1860's showed this information on the bottle labels. In 1861 the house became the official supplier of Champagne to Queen Victoria and later to the French Imperial court. By the 1920's Perrier-Jouet was exporting around 3/4 million bottles a year to the UK.

Emile Gallé took over from Charles and he commissioned a master glassmaker to decorate a magnum for the House's quality vintage. Years later the decoration called Belle Epoque, of white anemones and enamelled roses circled with gold became the house distinctive emblem.

In 1959, Perrier-Jouet and its sister Champagne House G.H.Mumm became part of the Canadian Seagram group but is now owned by Allied Domecq Group.

Champagne Houses

Pierre Garbais **Aube 5**
13 rue du Pont
Celles sur Ource
Tel: 00 33 (0)325 38 51 29
www.gerbais.com
Open daily. Tours with detailed explanation of the production of champagne are available by appointment.
Getting There: Just before leaving the village there is a bridge. Turn left here.
Pierre Gerbais has 14ha of mostly Pinot Noir and Chardonnay vines but there is some Pinot Meunier and an old variety called old Pinot Blanc. All their wines are produced in-house in their family 'pressoir'. Their range of wines start at 11 euros for the Tradition to 18,30 euros for the L'Originale, an unusual champagne made entirely of the old Pinot Blanc grape variety. This makes L'Originale a very rare champagne that must be tasted and that alone makes a visit to this house worthwhile.

Piper-Heidsieck **Marne 1**
51 Boulevard Henry Vasnier
Reims 51100
Tel: 00 33 (0)325 84 43 00
Open daily
Tours are offered regularly in an electric car, with English commentary. The gift shop sells champagne as well as other items.
Cost: 6 euros includes a glass of champagne or 10 euros for the "Prestige" tour and you get to taste three champagnes.
The Heidsieck part of the Piper-Heidsieck winery has been around since 1785 when a former cloth maker, Florens-Louis Heidsieck, went to Reims and discovered wine.

When Florens-Louis Heidsieck died in 1828 his nephew Christian Heidsieck took over in partnership with his cousin Henri Guillaume Piper thus creating Piper-Heidsieck dynasty. It wasn't until 1997 that the familiar red colour was used in their logo.

Since then Piper Heidsieck has managed to become the official Champagne of the Cannes Film festival and is marketed with as much

Champagne Houses

celebrity and pomp as it can muster. Images of celebrities such as Russel Crowe and Kim Basinger enjoying their fizz adorn the walls of their lobby and Marilyn Monroe claimed that a glass of Piper each morning spread a little warmth throughout her body. Even Jean Paul Gaultier has aligned himself with Piper and 'dressed' the wine in a vibrant fire engine red vinyl corset woven together with black lace. The tour itself has hints of Hollywood about it.

Visitors are taken on tour in an electric car which passes through various galleries whose walls are sculpted with images or harvesters and bunches of grapes evoking the story of Champagne production. There are even some special effects including a strobe lit gallery with floating bubbles. This is partnered with a recorded commentary.

Pommery Marne 1

5 place du Général Gouraud
Reims
Tel: 00 33 (0)326 61 62 56
www.pommery.com

Tours, available in English, include the cellars and vineyards and each lasts around 45-60 minutes.
Cost: 8 euros pp

Located south of the city centre, the Pommery champagne house is renowned for producing some of the finest cuvées in Champagne, The winery's beautiful, expansive building has a neogothic monastic look about it - a reflection of the area's Gothic heritage.

It was founded by Alexandre Louis Pommery in 1858 but he died soon after and left it in the capable hands of Madame Pommery. In the 1860s she linked 20 chalk quarries that had been carved into the hills by the Romans in the second century. This formed a series of conical shaped champagne cellars that stretches for eleven miles and hold a dizzying twenty million bottles.

In order to ensure a regular

Champagne Houses

supply of quality grapes, Madame Pommery purchased some great vineyards in 1865.

Today, Pommery is considered to have one of the finest vineyards in the Champagne region. Their 300 acres of vines are all classed at one hundred per cent on the quality scale.

The Pommery style is fruity, elegant and with inherent lightness on the palate achieved by fermentation in steel tanks.

Their Pommery Brut Royal tends to be very popular. It's aged in cellars for three years and is a blend of 40 selected crus of the three Champagne grape varieties: Chardonnay, Pinot Noir and Meunier.

Theirs is a walking tour with a live guide who walks you down the magnificent 116 step staircase and into a maze of galleries and through the production process. The various chambers are named after areas where vast quantities of the wine were sold such as Bristol, Liverpool and Manchester.

Remy Massin & Fils Aube 13

Grande Rue
Ville Sur Arce
Tel: 00 33 (0)325 38 74 09

Tours are available by appointment. They include an explanation of production followed by a tasting.
The story starts with Aristide Massin planting the first vines. The vineyards were then created and cultivated by his son Marius Massin and his son, Rémy, in turn created the house and the brand in 1974. Rémy's son Sylvère Massin, has modernised by introducing state of the art thermo tanks to control fermentation and flavours.

They have twenty acres of vineyards and produce around 150,000 bottles of bubbly a year of five different styles: Prestige (a mix of Pinot Noir and Chardonnay), Millésime, Tradition (100% Pinot Noir comes in brut and demi-sec and extra brut), Rosé and Réserve. Their wines regularly win accolades and medals.

Champagne Houses

Ruinart Marne I
4 rue de Crayères
Reims
Tel: 00 33 (0)326 77 51 52
Tours are available by written appointment only but will include a visit to their excellent crayères (cellars).
Ruinart was established in 1729 by Dom Thierry Ruinart - a contemporary of Dom Pérignon) a year after Louis IV allowed the transport of wine in bottles. Though still wine was widely available Ruinart has the accolade of being the first recorded Champagne house, that is the first to establish themselves as a house selling bubbly wine.

This was remarkable because he started trading first in linen goods using champagne as a marketing incentive for customer loyalty. However, he received orders for the wine and eventually trading in champagne became more profitable. By the time his grandson, Jean-Irénée took over, the house was selling its wares to the King of Spain, King of Naples and Talleyrand and also to the Empress Josephine. Jean Irénée was himself ennobled as Vicomte de Brimont by Louis XVIII.

Ruinart's spectacular Gallo-Roman chalk pit cellars, located more than 30 metres below ground are officially classified as a historical monument

Ruinart was bought by Moët et Chandon in 1963 but still manages to maintain a great quality wine at great value prices. Its most famous wine is probably Dom Ruinart, which is always a vintage wine. It is made from 100% Chardonnay and offers a range of exotic fruits on the palate.

Taittinger Marne I
9 place Saint-Nicaise
Reims
Tel: 00 33 (0)326 85 83 33
www.taittinger.com
**Open daily during mid March to Mid November from 9.30am-1.00pm & 2pm-5.30pm. Other times open Mon.-Fri. only.
Closed bank holidays and Sun.
Tours, available in English, include the cellars and vineyards and each lasts**

Champagne Houses

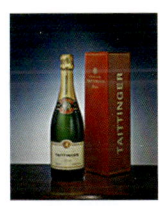

around 60 minutes. A film is shown just before the tour. A charge is applicable.

In 1734 a champagne merchant, Fourneaux, established Fourneaux-Forest, a company which formed the foundations of Taittinger. He was selling the wines that the Benedictine Abbeys of Hautvillers, Pierry, Verzy and Saint-Nicaise were producing. Success meant that after the WWI the company moved to a 13th century historical residence on rue de Tambour known as "the House of the Counts of Champagne".

This is where Thibaud IV lived. He brought back from Cyprus the vines which today create the king of grapes, Chardonnay.

Soon after a merger took place between Fourneaux-Forest and the Taittinger family who eventually took control.

It was Pierre Taittinger who decided that Chardonnay should be the dominant grape for the brand, giving the wines lightness, finesse and elegance.

Pierre's three sons began operation in the cellars of the Saint-Nicaise monastery built on Gallo-Roman chalk cellars dating from the 2nd century. The Abbey was destroyed in the French Revolution but there are still well preserved remnants.

The house is now in the hands of Claude Taittinger making this one of the few family owned Champagne Houses in the region.

The family cultivates an area of 280 hectares of vineyards spread across the best crus of the Champagne area. Their famous champagne the Comtes de Champagne label, is their most prestigious and only produced in exceptional years.

In 1987 the house founded Domaine Carneros in association with Kobrand Corporation in Napa Valley, California. They have an 83.4% stake in this company.

Champagne Houses

Veuve Clicquot Ponsardin

Marne 1

1 place des Droits-de-l'Homme
Reims
Tel: 00 33 (0)326 89 53 90
www.veuve-clicquot.com

Open Mon.-Sat. 1st April -31st October 10am-6pm.
Open Mon.-Fri. 10am-6pm 1st November to 31st March
Tours, available in English, include the family history, cellars and galleries and a film about the widow Clicquot is shown. This is followed by a tasting. Lasts around 90 minutes.

This house was first established in 1772 by wine merchant Philippe Clicquot and by 1775 it was the first to distribute rosé champagne. Philipe's son François Clicquot took over the business in 1779 but died of a fever in 1805 leaving his 27 year old widow Barbe Nicole Ponsardin to pick up the pieces. Veuve (widow) Clicquot took the reigns with much panache and success and is heralded as one of the most impressive business women in modern times. By 1810 the house became known as Veuve Clicquot Ponsardin and created its first vintage wine.

Thanks to her, the process of remuage (riddling - a way of turning the bottles so that the sediment is drawn out) became part of the method of champagne production.

When Veuve Clicquot died some 60 years later, she had became known as the Grande Dame of Champagne.

The most famous Champagne is the yellow label most enjoyed for its freshness and vitality.

Champagne Houses

Vranken Marne 16

42 ave de Champagne
Epernay
Tel: 00 33 (0)326 59 50 50
www.vranken.net

**Open Mon-Thur. 9am-11.30am and 2pm-6pm. April to Jan open Sat 9.30am-12pm and 2pm-4.30pm
No appointment necessary.
Cost: 3,50 euros per person with a tasting included.**

Paul-François Vranken, the President of Vranken, arrived in Champagne during the seventies with the ambitious intention of creating a Champagne House.

The Vranken brand was created in 1976 and thereafter a series of acquisitions including Veuve Monnier in 1978, Charles Lafitte & Cie in 1983, Champagne Sacotte in 1987, Champagne Lallement of Bouzy in 1992 Heidsieck & Co Monopole in 1996, Pommery & Greno in 2002 has made this company huge. The Demoiselle brand was their own creation born in 1985.

They can boast that they are the second biggest Champagne firm in the world and that their products are consumed in over eighty countries.

For the visiting consumer to Vranken, all this means you are spoilt for choice.

The visit begins around a model of the vineyard locating the different structures of the house and a look at the painted windows depicting fashion. This is followed by a trip down to the cellar for a sound and light show in a vaulted room. Once back on the ground floor a wine tasting offering a variety of champagnes is on offer. These include Piper Heidsieck & Co, Charles Laffitte, Demoiselle (note the fantastic bottles).

Gastronomy

Large areas of Champagne have traditionally been a game hunter's paradise. So regional cuisine has traditionally been rustic and hearty.

Though Champagne does not have its own trademark dishes, you can find almost all types of French cuisine in Champagne's restaurants, especially the specialities of Lorraine, Burgundy, Northern France and a great deal of simple but inspired Flemish cuisine.

Nevertheless, the region's most popular dishes reflect the variety of products that are naturally available within its borders. For instance, France's largest game hunting ground, **Arc-en Barrois**, is located in Champagne and so the mix of regional cuisines includes a veritable selection of charcuterie - game - such as venison and wild boar (sanglier) which are prepared as roasts or casseroles or in a potée champenoise (stew from the Champagne region). This can include up to five different meats and several vegetables in the same dish.

The forests of Ardennes have an abundance of edible offerings that make their way onto menus. Jambon des Ardennes - a cold-cured ham, is generally eaten as an appetiser and may be included in many dishes. So are the different mushrooms such as cèpes, morels and chanterelles.

Roast rabbit or roast thrush are also regional favourites. These are also sometimes served up in rich patés and terrines and flavoured with juniper berries. Most peculiarly,

> Perhaps Champagne has enough on its plate with its wine production. When it comes to food, it simply borrows the cuisine from its neighbours!

Gastronomy

pigs trotters also make an appearance especially in Sainte Ménehould in the Marne region where they can be boiled, stewed or barbecued..

If you see dishes on the menu with names that are almost impossible to pronounce, such as Pot'je vleesch or Flamiche aux Zermezeelois, you can be sure that these are of Flemish origin. Ingredients such as prunes, raisins, brown sugar, chicory and beer (especially Bière des Trois Monts) find their way into much of the Flemish cooking - a sure sign that Belgium is nearby.

Flamiche au Maroilles, a creamy very flavoursome quiche, is probably the most famous cheese dish of Northern France. Many a cheese tart is made with it, served both hot and cold.

One example is the flamkuche. This has a crusty base topped with melted cheese, as well as onions and *lardons* - small pieces of ham and quite often with leeks too. When it has been served, roll it up and eat it with your fingers. Most restaurants will offer Flemish dishes, distinguishable by their tongue twisting names. Andouilles and andouillettes - chitterling sausages - especially from Troyes, Arras and Cambrai, are savoured and eaten with potatoes and cabbage.

Seafood is not as prevalent as meat dishes, but cod, Dover sole, mussels from Boulogne and cockles from Picardy are all found on Champenoise menus. In particular matelote champenoise is popular. It is salted or pickled herring generally served as an appetiser with potatoes. Other variations could be hareng saur - a smoked herring or hereng bouffi - a salted and smoked herring.

As the region has a cool climate, the vegetables that accompany the main meal tend to be cabbage, potato, beets, watercress, Belgian endive and leek - all vegetables which prosper in this sort of climate.

Gastronomy

Suggestions for Sublime Champagne & food combinations

Romance
Try invoking some romance with black winter truffles and a bottle of Blanc de Noirs Champagne.

Pure Indulgence
Foie Gras, whether goose or duck both have creamy beige or ivory tones and silky smooth textures. But they taste quite different.

Goose Foie Gras
This is both soft and smooth and should be matched with a light lively Blanc de Blancs Champagne - ideally match with a Brut or extra-Brut champagne.

Duck Foie Gras
This is quite rustic and will be superb with most champagnes.

Part Cooked Duck Foie Gras
Eat with a fresh crusty loaf and match it with a mature champagne made with Pinot Noir and Pinot Meunier grapes.

Family Lunch
Sunday roasts with game or poultry are perfect with champagnes produced with 100% black grapes such as Pinot Noir or Pinot Meunier thanks to these wines' powerful bouquet and good structure.

Menu Guide

The word 'gourmand(e)' refers to someone who loves eating good food. If this is you and you would like to take your tastes buds on an adventure, this section is for you.

Note: Restaurants generally open between 12-2.30pm for lunch and again between 6pm-10.30pm for dinner.

Andouille
A big pork, chitterling and tripe sausage. Served cold.

Andouillette
This is a pork, chitterling and tripe sausage which is grilled and served hot. This dish originates from Arras and Cambrai areas and is served with fries.

Anges à Cheval
'Angels on horseback' refers to grilled oysters wrapped in bacon.

Anguille Au Vert
Sauteed eel cooked in green herbs, spinach, sorrel and wine sauce. It is served on fried bread.

Arc on ciel
Rainbow trout

Beef Carpaccio & Foie Gras
This is a popular combination of beef with ducks liver

Boudin Blanc
A white pudding style sausage poached in a sauce or wine.

Boudin de Lapin
A black sausage made from rabbit meat.

Boudin Noir
Black pudding.

Cahuse or Caqhuse
Pork braised with onions.

Carré d'agneau
Loin of Lamb

Coq à la Bière
This chicken stew

Menu Guide

L'Escargot
This quintessentially French delicacy is found on many a menu in Champagne. However, die hard snail lovers can always visit the snail farms to feed their addiction. There is one in Olizy near Reims and another in Bernon located between Troyes and Auxerre.

Musée de L'Escargot
Olizy Violaine
30km west of Reims by junction 21 on the A4 to Paris
t: 00 33 321 26 58 10 77
Visits by appointment.
This is run by Marie-Françoise and the tour of the hatchery and nursery lasts around 1 hour.

La Fontaine de Bernne
Bernon, between Troyes and Auxerre
T: 00 33 325 70 08 34.
Visits by appointment
This establishment is famed for producing the world's largest snail cassolette.

is cooked in beer and juniper gin and prepared with mushrooms.

Carbonnade à la Flamande
A popular beef stew dish based on thinly sliced beef, slow-cooked for three hours in beer and onion then sweetened with brown sugar.

Chateaubriand
A piece of beef fillet

L'Escargot
Snails are famous through France and are usually cooked in lots of garlic, parsley and melted butter.

Faisan à la Flamande
Pheasant cooked in beer.

Ficell picard
Ham and mushroom pancake served with Bechamel sauce

Flamiche or flamique
This is the Flemish word for cake and can be sweet or

A Menu Guide

savoury. The best known is made with leeks or pumpkins, and sometimes Maroilles cheese.

Gaufres à la Citrouille
A deep fried pumpkin waffle cooked with vegetables and rum.

La Goyère au Carré de Vinage
A rich cheese pie served hot.

Hochepot
This is a filling Flemish style stew. A mixture of beef, lamb, veal, pork, pigs ears and oxtails, with cabbage and root vegetables, herbs and spices. The word hochepot is an old French word meaning "to shake". The English word hodgepodge is derived from this. The dish Pot-au-feu is the same but the meat has not been browned first.

Jambon d'Ardennes
A lovely rose coloured cold smoked ham from Ardennes. It is generally eaten as an appetiser sometimes with local pickles.

Pieds de Cochon
The best pigs' trotters in Champagne must be those found in Champagne's Pig Trotter capital Sainte Ménehould. This is a small town located 60km east of Reims. Unlike Reims, its most famous produce is pigs' trotters (pieds de cochon). The story goes that the glutinous version of the dish was invented here when someone left the pot cooking overnight by mistake. For over 200 years chefs throughout Sainte Ménehould have been guarding their own recipes for the dish. Restaurants also serve pigs' ears and pigs' tails. If you want to buy some pieds de cochons, head for the town's local trotters boutique,

Au Pied de Cochon
Tel: 00 33 (0)326 60 17 71

The **Confrérie Gastronomique des Compagnons du Pied d'Or** - gastronomic brotherhood of the golden trotter - is located at **Auberge du Soleil d'Or**
Tel: 00 33 (0)3 26 60 82 49

A Menu Guide

Lapin au Pruneaux
Rabbit cooked with prunes. This dish has its origins in Poland but is widely embraced as a typically Flemish dish.

Lapin de garenne Valenciennes
Wild rabbit, stewed with prunes and raisins.

Langue Lucullus
This dish is a mix of foie gras (duck liver) and smoked tongue.

Matelote Champenoise
Salted or pickled herrings served with potatoes.

Pâté de Canard
A duck pâté from Amiens.

Pieds de Cochon
Pigs Trotters, mainly found in Sainte Ménehould.

Pigeonneau
Pigeon is often found on Flemish menus.

Champagne Sauce
Unsurprisingly, many dishes will be served with a Champagne sauce. In case you are wondering, the ingredients are:
butter, flour, chicken stock, heavy cream and of course champagne.

Potée Champenoise
A stew from the champagne region usually a mix of five meats including beef and a variety of vegetables.

Potjevleesch
Probably the most popular Flemish dish, potjevleesch originates from Dunkerque and comprises a terrin of three meats, veal, pork and rabbit or chicken, duck and rabbit. The meat is cooked with onions, garlic and white wine, lemon and tomatoes and served in a golden jelly. It is eaten cold and sometimes served with French fries or just a simple salad.

A Menu Guide

Le Poulet au Maroilles
A pungent dish comprising chicken cooked in the strong Maroilles cheese.

Smakeluk
Rabbit cooked in beer

Soupe à l'Ail
This is garlic soup. A speciality of Douai.

Soup à la Bière
Soup made with cream, beer and onions.

Tarte au Fromage
also known as
Flamiche au Zermezeelois
This is a cheese tart - usually made with Maroille cheese - served warm and generally accompanied with salad or French fries The word Flamiche is the Flemish word for 'cake' or 'flan'. The most popular flamiche is made with leeks.

Sanglier
Wild Boar served either roasted or as a pâté or terrine with juniper berries.

Soup à la Biere/au Potiron
Soup made with beer, cream and onion/with pumpkin

Tarte au Queumeu
A quiche made from Langres cheese martured with Marc de Champagne.

Tatin de Canard aux Pommes
Layered duck tart with apples.

Veau Flamande
A sweet tasting dish of Veal cooked with dried apricots, prunes and raisins.

Waterzoi
This refers to a dish of either mixed freshwater fish such as a carp or poultry such as chicken. It is cooked with vegetables and cream and served in a thick spicy sauce.

Cheese

CHEESE (FROMAGE) OF CHAMPAGNE

No self respecting French region would forget to produce cheese. Here's a selection for your cheeseboard.

Fromage Blanc cream cheese

Barberey
This soft white salted cheese, made from skimmed milk is also known as **Fromage de Troyes** and is somewhat reminiscent of Camembert. It derives its name from a village near Troyes called Barberey. It is produced by small farms and churned out as a flat disc, is coated in ashes and boxed. It gives off a slightly musty aroma. It is best eaten between July and November.

Caprice des Dieux
This commercially made oval shaped cheese is made from double cream. It has a downy rind and can be eaten all year.

Fromage Chèvre goats cheese

Carré de L'Est
Some might find this square shaped cheese a little bland and somewhat mushroomy on the nose. It can be eaten throughout the year.

Cendré des Riceys/Champagne
This soft, flat-disc skimmed-milk cheese is made by farms and small dairies. It has a rather nutty taste and is best eaten between July and November.

TIP: Cheese fanatics can visit **Musée du Fromage** in Chaorce, 30km south of Troyes
T: 00 33 325 40 10 67.
Closed Tues. entry 3 Euros

Cheese

Chaorce
This cheese melts in the mouth. It is one of the best AOC cow's milk cheeses of the area. It comes as a thick disc and has a nutty and sometimes flavoursome fruity taste, a white rind and mushroom aromas. Its texture ranges from pasty to runny depending on its age. Best between July and November but can be eaten even if not fully ripe. It is an ideal accompaniment Champagne!

Chaumont
This pungent cheese offers a spicy flavour in a small cone bundle. Made by farms and small dairies and best eaten between July and November.

Comte
A nutty flavoured cow's milk cheese also known as **Gruyere** its origins are neither French or Swiss but from Charlemagne's reign where forests were termed gruyeres.

Ervy-Le Châtel
A cone shaped mild cheese best between May and October.

Langres
Langres is another of Champagne's top notch AOC cow's milk cheeses. It has a tangy, pungent taste best between May and October. It has a hollow top where some pour **marc** (grape brandy) into before eating.

Maroilles
A famous cheese with its lovely orange crust from Northern France which has a very pungent aroma. It is washed in beer while ripening.

Mimolette
This strikingly orange coloured cheese is also known as **Boule de Lille** after the city of Lille where it was created. It is very much like a melon sized Edam. It has a natural rind that through time, roughens and becomes pockmarked.

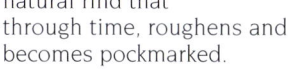

Trappiste de Igny
A large flat disc made by monks in Igny and best between May and October.

Menu Reader

A-Z of Miscellaneous Items on a French Menu

Le Viandes	Meat	Les Poissons	Fish
L'Agneau	Lamb	Anchois	Anchovy
Assiette Anglaise	Plate of cold meats	Anguille	Eel
Bifteck	Steak	Araignée	Spider Crab
Bifteck Haché	Hamburger	L'Assiette	Smoked Fish
Boeuf	Beef	Nordique	Platter
Carré d'Agneau	Rib of Lamb	Bar et Loup de Mer	Sea-wolf
Chevreuil	Venison		
Côtes d'Agneau	Lamb Chops	Barbe	Brill
Côte de Boeuf	Side of Beef	Bigorneau	Winkle
Côte de Porc	Pork Chop	Cabillaud	Fresh Cod
Côte de Veau	Veal	Carrelet et Plie	Plaice
Contrefilet	Sirloin	Colin	Hake
Entrecôte	Steak	Coquilles St-Jacques	Scallops St. Jacques
Faux Filet	Sirloin Steak		
Filet de Boeuf	Fillet of Beef	Crabes	Crabs
Foie	Liver	Crevette Grise	Shrimp
Foie de Veau	Calves' Liver	Crustacés	Shellfish
Gigot d'Agneau	Leg of Lamb	Dorade	Sea Bream
Jambon	Ham	Ecrevisses	Crayfish
Langue	Tongue	Escargots	Snails
Langue de Boeuf	Ox Tongue	Etrille	Swimming Crab
Lapereau	Young rabbit	Fléton fumé	Smoked halibut
Lapin	Rabbit	Fruit de Mer	Seafood
Lard Fumé	Smoked Bacon	Gamba	Large Prawn
Lièvre	Hare	Harengs	Herring
Porc	Pork	Homard	Lobster
Rognons	Kidneys	Limande	Lemon Sole
Saucisse	Sausage	Langouste	Spiny Lobster
Tête de Veau	Calves' Head	Langoustines	Norway Lobster

142

Menu Reader

Les Poissons	**Fish contd.**
Huître	Oyster
Lieu	Coal Fish
Limande	Lemon Sole
Lotte	Monkfish
Maquereau	Mackerel
Merlan	Whiting
Morue	Cod
Moules	Mussels
Oursins	Sea hedgehog
Péntoncle	Small Scallop
Praire	Clam
Raie	Skate
Rouget	Red Mullet
Royan	A large sardine
Salad Océan	Ocean Salad
Sandre	Pike-perch
Sardines	Sardines
Saumon	Salmon
Sole	Sole
Thon	Tuna
Truite (de Mer)	Trout (Sea)
Truite arc en ciel	Rainbow Trout
Turbot	Turbot

Volaille	**Poultry**
Bécasse	Woodcock
Caneton/Canard	Duck
Caille	Quail
Dindon	Turkey
Oie	Goose
Faisan	Pheasant
Foie Gras	Duck Liver pâté
Foie Volaille	Chicken Liver
Magret Canard	Duck Fillet
Perdreau	Partridge
Pigeon	Pigeon
Pintarde	Guinea-fowl
Poulet	Chicken
Poularde	Boiled Chicken
Poussin	Spring Chicken
Ris de Veau	Veal sweetbread

Sauce	**Sauce**
Béarnaise	Sauce made from egg yolks, shallots, wine and tarragon
Béchamel	White sauce with herbs
Beurre Blanc	Loire sauce with butter, wine and shallots
Beurre Noir	Blackened butter
Meunière	Butter and lemon sauce

Oeufs	**Eggs**
- Coque	- Boiled
- mollet	- soft boiled
- Brouillés	- Scrambled
- Pochés	- Poached
- Oeufs sur le plat	- Fried eggs

Eating Out - Menu Reader

Fruit & Vegetables and Miscellaneous Items

Abricots	Apricots	Datte	Date
Amandes	Almonds	Eau	Water
Ananas	Pineapple	Endives	Chicory
Araignée	Spider-crab	Epinards	Spinach
Artichaut	Artichoke	Estragon	Tarragon
Asperge	Asparagus	Farée	Stuffed cabbage
Aubergines	Aubergines	Farine	Flour
Avocat	Avocado	Fenouil	Fennel
Barbadine	Passion fruit	Fenugrec	Fenugreek
Barbe de Capucin	Wild Chicory	Fèves	Broad beans
	Woodcock	Ficelle	shorter thin baguette
Betteraves	Beetroot	Figues	Figs
Beurre	Butter	Flageolets	Kidney Beans
Carottes	Carrots	Fraises	Strawberry
Céleri	Celery	Framboises	Raspberries
Cerises	Cherries	Fruit	Fruit
Champignons	Mushrooms	Gingembre	Ginger
Châtaignes	Chestnuts	Girofle	Clove
Chicorée	Chicory	Grenouilles	Frogs
Choux Bruxelle	Brussel Sprout	Groseilles	Currants
Chou Rouge	Red Cabbage	Harricots Verts	French Beans
Chou vert	Kale	Infusion	Herb teas
Choux Fleurs	Cauliflowers	Laitue	Lettuce
Citron	Lemon	Legumes	Vegetables
Concombre	Cucumber	Limon	Lime
Courgettes	Courgette	Mange Tous	Sugar pea
Crêpes	Pancakes	Mangue	Mango
Cresson	Cress	Mais	Sweet Corn
Croustade	Tartlets	Mandarines	Mandarines
Crudités	Raw vegetables		

144

Eating Out - Menu Reader

Marron	Chestnut
Melon	Melon
Navets	Turnips
Noisettes	Hazelnuts
Noix	Walnuts
Oignons	Onions
Oseille	Sorrel
Pastèque	Water Melon
Pêches	Peaches
Petits Pois	Green Peas
Pissenlits	Dandelions
Poire	Pear
Poivre	Pepper
Poireaux	Leeks
Poivrons rouges	Red Pepper
Poivrons Verts	Green Pepper
Pomme de Terre	Potato
Pomme	Apple
Potage	Soup
Prunes	Plum
Pruneau	Prunes
Radis	Radishes
Railfort	Horse Radish
Raisins	Grapes
Reine-Claude	Greengages
Riz	Rice
Salade	Salad
Sel	Salt
Suprême	Chicken breast or game bird
Tomates	Tomatoes

How is it cooked/served

Ballottine	Boned and rolled
Beignet	Deep fried in batter
Brandad	Creamy
Brandad du Nord	Mashed Potatoe
Braisé	Braised
Brochette	Skewer
Brouillade	Stew with oil
Chapelure	Breadcrumbs
Compote	Stewed (usually fruit)
Consommé	Clear soup
Coulis de..	Sauce of..
Crapaudine	Cooked fowl, split down the centre flattened and frilled.
Croustillant	Crispy or crunchy
Cuisse de..	Leg or thigh of..
Cuit au Four	Baked
En Branche	Vegetables served whole
Etoffé	Stuffed
Faisandé	Game that has been hung
Famille	Simple Cooking
Farci	Smoked
Fumé	Stuffed
Gratinée	Grill browned
Grillé	Grilled
Rôti	Roasted
Terrine	Coarse paté
Tornedos	Small round fillets

Menu Reader

Sweet Tooth?

Biscuits de Reims	Thin macaroons biscuits	Pommes au Four	Oven baked apples
Congolais	Coconut biscuits		
Créme aux oeufs	Custard	Rabote aka Talibur	Whole apple cooked in a pastry case
Gâteau battu aka kokeboterom	Like brioche with currants.		
Gaufres	Waffles with sugar & cream.	Raffolait	A blend of milk and boiled sugar with a caramel consistency often served with pancakes
Crème Glacée	Ice cream		
Massepain	Marzipan		
Nougat de Miel	Nougat made with honey.		
Mousse au Chocolate	Chocolate moose	Ris au Lait	Rice pudding
Pain d'épice	Gingerbread	Sorbet	Sorbet
Poire Belle-Hélène	Pear Belle-Hélène	Sucre	Sugar

Coffee Styles -
be specific about the kind of coffee you would like to have:

Un café, s'il vous plaît
You will receive an espresso coffee, strong and black in a small espresso cup.

Un café au lait s'il vous plaît
You will receive an espresso coffee with milk on the side.

Une crème s'il vous plaît
You will receive a small white coffee.

Une crème grande s'il vous plaît
You will receive a white coffee served in a normal size cup.

Restaurants

Here are some tried and tested restaurants. Tariffs are quoted in euros and are approximate.

ARDENNES
Charleville-Mézières

Au Cochon Qui Louche
31 rue Victor-Cousin
Charleville-Mézières
Located quite near Place Ducal.
Tel: 00 33 (0)3 24 35 49 05
Tariff: From 14 euros
Closed: Sun. eve & Mon
Cuisine: Traditional French
A convivial restaurant with a simple menu ideal for lunch or casual get-togethers.

La Côte à l'Os
11, Cours Aristide Briand
Charleville-Mézières
Tel: 00 33 (0)3 24 59 20 16
Tariff: From 20 euros
Cuisine: Traditional seafood
A well regarded brasserie style restaurant with a broad range of seafood as well as game dishes between. There is a tavern on the first floor

La Clef des Champs
33 rue du Moulin
Charleville-Mézières
In the town centre
Tel: 00 33 (0)3 24 56 17 50
Tariff: From 15-30 euros
Closed: Sun. pm & Mon
Cuisine: Traditional
A very friendly service within elegant surroundings. Seasonal and regional food especially game and fresh water fish.

ARDENNES
Givet

Maison Baudoin
2 place du 148e-Régiment
Givet
Located near the bridge
Tel: 00 33 (0)3 24 42 00 70
Tariff: From 14-47 euros
Closed: Sun. eve & Mon
Cuisine: Traditional
A chic restaurant with three rooms, decorated in light tones with timbered beams.

Restaurants

ARDENNES
Rethel

Au Sanglier des Ardennes
1 rue Pierre Curie
Rethel
Tel: 00 33 (0)3 24 38 45 19
Tariff: From 8 euros
Open: Daily
Cuisine: Traditional
Great restaurant and easy on the pocket.

ARDENNES
Sedan

La Crêperie du Château
10 place du Château
Sedan
Located opposite the fortified castle.
Tel: 00 33 (0)3 22 08 49
Tariff: From 15 euros
Closed: Sun. eve
Cuisine: Crêperie
On sunny days this crêperie offers agreeable seating on the terrace. Wash down your crêpe with a glass of cider.

La Ferme de Landi
Carrefour de Bellevue
Sedan
Located 2km out of town at the turn off for Vouziers
Tel: 00 33 (0)3 24 22 22 22
Tariff: From 8 euros
Closed: Tues pm & Wed.
Cuisine: Traditional
A lovely large house in a medieval setting serving Ardenne ham and seafood.

Aux Bon Vieux Temps
3 Place Halle
Sedan
From the station go down the long boulevard to the old cenre.
Tel: 00 33 (0)3 24 29 03 70
Tariff: From 15 euros
Closed: Sun. pm Mon.
Cuisine: Regional dishes
Stylish restaurant. Rabbit is served with prunes and jambon d'Ardennes is served with melon. Seafood appetizers superb. Lobster soufflé, salmon ravioli and langoustine gratin are three examples of regular menu items.

Restaurants

MARNE
Reims

Le Millénaire
4 rue Bertin,
Reims

Centrally located next to the tourist office and the cathedral.
Tel: 00 33 (0)3 26 08 26 62
Tariff: From £18.00
Closed: Sun., Sat. lunchtime
Cuisine: Gastronomic

This gastronomic restaurant is famous locally for its seafood, including roasted lobster. The menu also has a range of eight meat dishes with veal, beef and lamb where mustard and wine are used to flavour the dishes (see image of seabream which has been cooked with le Grand Cuvée Charles VII Brut). Appetizers include a range of foie gras preparations.

Boyer - Les Crayères
64 bd Henry Vasnier
Reims -

A short drive out of town via the Pommery Champagne house
Tel: 00 33 (0)3 26 82 80 80
Tariff: From £18.00
Closed: Sun
Cuisine: Its three Michelin stars make this Reims' finest restaurant. The vast menu covers all the great and good in French and local ingredients such as lobster, langoustine, foie gras, duck and seabass. Champagne and countless other flavours are elegantly combined to form the extravagant dishes. Classic interior dining together with one of the finest outdoor terrace's in France. Most of the guestrooms are opulent, traditional and individually styled. One or two are rather racy with leopard print covers.

Restaurants

La Vigneraie
11 rue Brûlart
Reims
Tel: 00 33 (0)3 26 88 67 27
Tariff: From 25 euros
Closed: Sun. day, Mon. Wed. lunchtime and August
Cuisine: Five gastronomic set menus to suit all budgets. Fish dominates the à la carte range with the carpaccio of scallops, tuna and salmon all in one dish as a speciality. A novel and relatively gamey meat section includes steaks with pistachio and Basque sauces, as well as with citrus fruit confits. Carpaccio of pineapple is one of several truly elegant desserts.

Les Charmes
11 rue Brûlart
Reims
Tel: 00 33 (0)3 26 85 37 63
Tariff: From 14 euros
Closed: Sun., Sat lunchtime

Cuisine: A gastronomic restaurant decked out in wood and decorated with works of art. The menu offers a mix of fruit, truffles, cream, lemon and wine along with the small number of meat and fish main courses. Salmon and rabbit are the house's speciality meats. Seafood appears heaviest as an appetizer. Scallops, salmon and langoustine are blended with fresh herbs and light sauces. Set menus are made up from diners' choices from the à la carte display. They also have a menu of around twenty whiskies.

Le Forêt Noire
2 bd Jules César
Reims
Tel: 00 33 (0)3 26 47 63 95
Tariff: From 14 euros
Cuisine: This petite restaurant serves Alsacian cuisine which includes around 10 tarte flambées served salads. Set menus include snail dishes and a Gewurtztraminer sorbet which

Restaurants

should all be washed down with their selection of Alsation wines.

Da Nello
39 rue Cérès
Reims
Tel: 00 33 (0)3 26 47 33 25
Tariff: From 12 euros
Cuisine: Italian restaurant serving Italian charcuteries and pizza. They have an award winning selection of Italian meat and fish dishes and a small selection of French and Italian wines.

Les Thiers
2 rue Thiers
Reims
Tel: 00 33 (0)3 26 40 23 48
Tariff: From 8 euros
Cuisine: This inexpensive bar/restaurant is the local hangout serving regional beers and wines. Dishes include steak and frites, steak tartare and Breton galettes with blé noir.

Brasserie du Boulingrin
48 rue de Mars,
Reims
Tel: Tariff: From 8 euros
Cuisine: Burgundy specials backed up by a wealth of wine from the famed region. Snails, rabbit terrine and steak tartare make up a few examples. The large meat miscellany includes veal, lamb and andouillette de Troyes. All of the latter items come grilled. Most of them are served with a pot of local mustard. The seafood selection is also impressive

Le Monté Cristo
3 rue de l'Ecu
Reims
Tel: 03 26 88 99 01
Tariff: From 8 euros
Cuisine: Dine at a table or by the bar choosing dishes such as beef with sauerkraut and steak tartar. Or go for a tapas with Serano ham, tomato, salad and prawns.

Restaurants

MARNE
Épernay

Les Berceaux
13 rue des Berceaux
Épernay
Tel: 00 33 (0)3 26 55 28 84
Tariff: From 20 euros
Closed: Tue. 15 Feb-2 Mar
Cuisine: Elegant and elaborate menu with local and more far flung specialities abound. Pigs' trotters, local ham with artichokes and foie gras share the menu with gazpacho soup, carpaccio of tuna and Breton galette crepes.

Au Bacchus Gourmet
21 rue Gambetta
Épernay
Tel: 00 33 (0)3 26 51 11 44
Tariff: From 20 euros
Closed: Mon, Tue.
Cuisine: Innovation blends with a few classic styles. Find carpaccio of lobster on Chinese noodles and guinea fowl tagliatelle mixing with ox tongue salad and seabass in olive pastry. Several of the dishes take influence from beyond France's borders, a rarity in the region, such as the carpaccio of beef with lemon and the grilled trout with aged Parmesan on top. Or how about pigs trotters with roasted peanuts? The hundred plus bottles of wine on offer is a reason to visit alone.

Le St Vincent
22 rue de Reims
Épernay
Tel: 00 33 (0)3 26 51 80 41
Tariff: From 15 euros
Closed: Sun day, Mon. day, Tue day.
Cuisine: Serious restaurant with two solid set menus, the least expensive being half the price of the other. Lighter items include aioli-smeared langoustine, seafood brochettes and andouillette de Troyes.

Restaurants

Heavier offerings range from the house cassoulet to the simply cooked slabs of beef.

Les Cépages
16 rue de la Fauvette
Épernay
Tel: 00 33 (0)3 26 55 16 93
Tariff: From 22 euros
Closed: Wed, Thu; 25 Dec–30 Dec.
Cuisine: A selection of menus with the most expensive featuring three Champagne-splashed dishes. The seafood is as extravagant as it comes, with sea bream in Champagne and John Dory with local mushrooms. The meat selection is a far more basic affair. Pigeon often features as an accompaniment to the pigs' trotters. The vast selection of wines and Champagnes stretch up to several hundred euros per bottle.

Le Chapon Fin
2 pl Mendès-France
Épernay
Located on the square close to the railway station.
Tel: 00 33 (0)3 26 55 40 03
Tariff: From 15 euros
Closed: 5–19 Mar.
Cuisine: A good value brasserie serving regional cuisine such as andouillette de Troyes and rabbit. There are some seafood dishes too.

La Cave à Champagne
16 rue Gambetta
Épernay
Tel: 00 33 (0)3 26 55 50 70
Tariff: From 22 euros
Closed: Wed day
Cuisine: A gastronomic restaurant but offering good value. They are so proud of their awards, they have displayed them outside the restaurant. Local ham is served in puff pastry and cassoulet with scallops. Stacks of Champagne too.

Restaurants

MARNE
CHÂLONS-EN-CHAMPAGNE

Le Petit Pasteur
42 rue Pasteur
Châlons-en-Champagne
Tel: 00 33 (0)3 26 68 24 78
Tariff: From 25 euros
Closed: Mon lunchtime, Sat lunchtime; Aug.
Cuisine: Foie gras is a house speciality at this traditional eatery. The small à la carte selection has simply but expertly cooked fish and meat dishes. Beef with sautéed potatoes and lamb with thyme both on offer. Appetizers include roasted goat's cheese with almonds and carpaccio of salmon.

Pré St Alpin
2 rue Abbé Lambert, 51000 Châlons-en-Champagne
Tel: 00 33 (0)3 26 70 20 26
Tariff: From 25 euros
Closed: Sun day.
Cuisine: Seafood selection served beneath a breathtaking raised ceiling. The quality here is superb. Brochettes come with scallops and prawns on. The simple carpaccio of beef and the duck dishes are particularly good. Over 40 bottles stud the wine list, with many reds from Burgundy and many whites from the Alsace.

Au Carrillon Gourmand
15 pl Monseigneur Tissier, 51000 Châlons-en-Champagne - 5 minutes on foot from the town centre
Tel: 00 33 (0)3 26 64 45 07
Tariff: From 15 euros
Closed: Sun day, Mon, Wed day.
Cuisine: The building may be bland but the seafood comes highly recommended. Scallops and prawns share a brochette. Some of the fishes are curried. Other creative dishes for the area include local vegetable gazpacho soup and aubergine caviar. More traditional is the meat selection with local mustard adding zest to several of the menu choices.

Restaurants

Le Chaudron Savoyard
9 rue des Poissoniers
Châlons-en-Champagne
Tel: 00 33 (0)3 26 68 00 32
Tariff: From 15 euros
Closed: Mon, Sat lunchtime
Cuisine: Plenty of raclettes laden with lard, spinach and potatoes. Solid show of regional cheeses. Charcuteries include platters of Ardennes and Champagne ham. Several salad options in the summer. Selection of filling tarts also.

Le Renard
24 pl de la République,
Châlons-en-Champagne
Tel: 00 33 (0)3 26 68 03 78
Tariff: From 22 euros
Closed: Sun day, Sat lunch; Christmas.
Cuisine: Three set menus with the most expensive being a stunning gastronomic display. Regional delights include snail brochettes and house foie gras. Seafood makes a strong showing with langoustines, fillets of red mullet and seabass served in intricate ways with pistachio nuts, citrus fruit and vegetables.

Restaurant de l'Avenue
86 ave de Sainte-Menehould,
Châlons-en-Champagne
10 minutes walk from the town centre
Tel: 00 33 (0)3 26 68 04 44
Tariff: From 15 euros
Closed: Sun day
Cuisine: There is New Zealand fish Hoki and kangaroo steaks on the à la carte menu and three set menus with Burgunday snails with local mustard and Champagne and cassoulet au fruits de mer both present.

Restaurant les Ardennes
34 pl de la République
Châlons-en-Champagne
Tel: 00 33 (0)3 26 68 21 42
Tariff: From 15 euros
Closed: Sun. day, Mon. day
Cuisine: Simple meat dishes cooked to perfection with a minimal number of trimmings. Bavettes, veal and lamb chops are served with shallots,

Restaurants

mushrooms and thyme respectively. The assiette au fruits de mer with scallops, clams and langoustine is a popular in the summer and oysters also plentiful in season.

Auberge du Cloitre
9 pl Notre-Dame
Châlons-en-Champagne
Tel: 00 33 (0)3 26 65 68 08
Tariff: From 15 euros
Closed: Mon. day, Tue.
Cuisine: Regional
Delectable meat assortment made up almost exclusively of beef and duck. Steak in a mussel sauce is just one incarnation of the former. Pigs' trotters also. Fondued red mullet fillets and salmon in a parsley sauce highlight the seafood menu. Solid array of red Burgundy wines.

MARNE
L'EPINE

Aux Armes de Champagne
ave de Luxembourg
L'Epine
Two motorways converge here. Exit 28 on A4/Exit 18 on A26 nr. to Châlons en Champagne
Tel: 00 33 (0)3 26 69 30 30
Tariff: Around 28 euros
Closed: Sun eve
Cuisine: Gastronomic food is served by 1 star michellin chef Philip Zeiger in an elegant dining room with views over the Gothic Notre-Dame d l'Epine Basiclica. The menu offers a balance of meat and fish dishes all served with panache and imagination. Try the Foie Gras served with vinegrette leeks or roasted turbot served with courgettes and potatoes.

Restaurants

AUBE
TROYES

L'Etoile
11 rue Pithou,
Troyes
Tel: 00 33 (0)3 25 73 12 65
Tariff: From 15 euros
Cuisine: Regional cooking including several variations of andouillette de Troyes. Platters of local cheese and herrings come up as appetizers. Omelettes are cooked with regional ham and Gruyère cheese. The ten or so wines contain some Alsace whites and Burgundy reds.

La Marinière
3 rue de la Trinité
Troyes
Tel: 00 33 (0)3 25 73 77 29
Tariff: From 8 euros
Closed: Sun.
Cuisine: About 40 different styles of mussels are served in an attractive pine kitted interior. Many come blended with Roquefort, cider, Calvados, sauerkraut or even Ricard pastis. Salmon and tuna are the main fishes served. Both come on brochettes, in pasta or simply with pepper and a slice of lemon. Pizzas by the dozen. Small seafood platters. and a lunchtime offer of any mussel dish, a plate of frites and a dessert for around £4.

Le Bistroquet
10 rue Louis Ulbach
Troyes
Tel: 00 33 (0)3 25 73 65 65
Tariff: From 28 euros
Closed: Sunday.
Cuisine: Regional
Pork, lamb, veal and beef each have their own menu and include. andouillette de Troyes, curried lamb, veal in a saltimbocca sauce and steak tartare.Two set menus offer gourmet dining at great prices. Fruits de mer risotto and roast seabass sum up the quality on offer. Modern, cool interior with a few signs of the its 19th century roots.

Restuarants

Chez Edouard
10 rue Kléber
Troyes
Tel: 00 33 (0)3 25 80 51 05
Tariff: From 25 euros
Closed: Sun day. Sat Lunch
Cuisine: Steak, salmon or a plate of foie gras will come with alcohol-based sauces to tomatoes, asparagus and nuts. Flambées appear on the small à la carte list. The gourmet set menu will probably include a lobster starter. Wines are by the carafe. The place is a little old fashioned yet charming.

Grenadine
16 rue Louis Ulbach
Troyes
Tel: 00 33 (0)3 25 73 74 22
Tariff: From 8 euros
Closed: Sun, Mon
Cuisine: Rustic Breton-style restuarant with a local twist. Galletes can be filled with ham, Gruyère cheese, snails and eggs. Flambées use Grand Marnier and Calvados and sweet crêpes can have honey, almond and pear fillings.

Le Soleil de l'Inde
33 rue de la Cité
Troyes
Tel: 00 33 (0)3 25 80 75 71
Tariff: From 14 euros
Closed: Mon
Cuisine: Indian cuisine. Each dish is carefully explained and can be eaten with nan, parata or roti breads. Every one of the meats and fish, including lamb, chicken and beef, is curried according to tikka, pakora or biryani methods. Huge choice for vegetarians.

Le Carpaccio
3 pl Langevin,
Troyes
Tel: 00 33 (0)3 25 73 31 10
Tariff: From 14 euros
Cuisine: Italian
Tagliatelle and spaghetti with salmon, chicken and fruits de mer. Pizzas have a French feel, with the Niçoise featuring olives, anchovies and egg. Simple meat offerings include andouillette de Troyes and peppered duck fillet.

Restuarants

HAUT MARNE
CHAUMONT

Palmier
34 rue Victor Mariette
Chaumont
Tel: 00 33 (0)3 25 32 67 22
Tariff: From 25-35 euros
Cuisine: Pizza
The pizza varieties here include fruits de mer, goat's cheese et al and are expertly made. The tiny range of meat dishes are grilled and simple. Bavettes come with shallots, steak with pepper and the lamb on brochettes.

Le Jardin
4 Félix Bablon
Chaumont
Tel: 00 33 (0)3 25 03 89 87
Tariff: From 25-25 euros
Closed: Sun, Mon
Cuisine: Regional
Brochettes of lamb, rump steaks and duck breasts are served with herbs, unelaborate cheese sauces and spices. Four set menus offer assiettes of local ham and cheese,

HAUT MARNE
COLOMBEY-LES-DEUX EGLISES

Auberge de la Montagne**
17 rue de la Montagne
Colombey-Les-Deux-Eglises
Tel: 00 33 (0)3 25 01 51 69
Tariff: 46-69 euros
Cuisine: Gastronomic
Michelin-starred restaurant combining ingredients from the sea, rivers and land to absolute perfection. Tarts, platters of cold meat and Langres cheese soften the palate for more. Small portions of lobster and seabass mix with pike and trout, each delicately prepared. Extremely classy considering the rural environment.

Restuarants

HAUT MARNE
LANGRES

Le Diderot
4 rue de l'Estres
Langres
Tel: 00 33 (0)3 25 87 07 00
Tariff: From 51-75 euros
Closed: 15 Nov-30th Nov.
Cuisine: French gastronomic
Le Diderot, highly regarded locally, is in the vaulted rooms of a Le Cheval Blanc hotel located in a former monastery. Lobster, veal and scallops are highly praised. Some dishes take influence from beyond France's borders, such as the Szechwan-style fillet of beef with figs. Most of the 15 or so wines are from Burgundy or Bordeaux.

Le Square
2 rue Général Leclerc
Langres
Tel: 00 33 (0)3 25 84 23 00
Tariff: From 36-50 euros
Closed: Mon.
Cuisine: French gastronomic
Opulent dining in an old stone townhouse by the church. The appetizers are spectacular. Carpaccio of duck and scallops on the same plate, crab and prawn terrine and salmon and caviar tartare to name just three. The regional set menu includes wine. Rabbit, nuts, honey and veal feature strongly on it. Langoustine in Noilly-Prat is yet another astounding dish.

Tarantella
10 rue Boulière
Langres
Tel: 00 33 (0)3 25 88 57 50
Tariff: From 25-35 euros
Closed: Sun.
Cuisine: Regional
Grilled meats are a little out of the ordinary with beef foristier-style and smotherings of cheese on some cuts. Andouillette de Troyes is served with Dijon mustard. The appetizers are tasty indeed with frogs' legs, smoked ham, snails, Langres cheese and several mussel dishes available.

Hotels

ARDENNES
Charleville-Mézières

**Le Relais du Square **
3 Place de la Gare
Charleville-Mézières
Tel: 00 33 (0)3 24 33 38 76
Tariff: 31-60 euros
Pleasant guestrooms close to the train station. En-suite bathrooms, satellite television and direct dial telephones are indicative of its two-star rating. Rooms are soundproofed against the outside noise. The wooden lobby and staircase are full of character. Public parking in the square outside the hotel.

Hôtel de Paris**
24 avenue G. Corneau
Charleville-Mézières
This hotel is located five minutes from the town centre opposite the station.
Tel: 00 33 (0)3 24 33 34 38
Tariff: 44-46 euros
A pleasant 29 room hotel.

ARDENNES
Givet

Hôtel le Val Saint-Hilaire**
6-7 quai des Fours
Givet
Located 1km from Givet town centre along the Meuse river.
Tel: 00 33 (0)3 24 42 38 50
Tariff: 56 euros
Closed: 20 Dec-5 Jan
A traditional 18th century hotel with comfortable rooms en-suite with television, telephone and hair drier. It has a secure car park and restaurant.

ARDENNES
Sedan

**Hôtel de l'Europe **
2 Place de la Gare, Sedan
next to Sedan station
Tel: 00 33 (0)3 24 27 18 71
Tariff: From 30 euros
Guests benefit from Internet access, a bar and private parking. Bedrooms have mod. cons: satellite television, direct dial telephones and the most modern bathrooms in town.

Hotels

ARDENNES
Signy-L'Abbaye

L'Auberge de L'Abbaye**
Place Aristide-Briand
Signy-L'Abbaye
Located in centre of village
Tel: 00 33 (0)3 52 81 27
Tariff: 38-56 euros
Closed: Jan-Feb
A charming inn style stone built hotel with eight bedrooms offering a tv, telephone and parking. It's gastronomic restaurant serves delicious food using farm produce and garden vegetables.

Getting there: From Reims take RN51, left Rethel then D985

ARDENNES
Vouziers

Argonne Hotel **
Route de Reims
Vouziers
Tel: 00 33 (0)324 71 42 14
Tariff: From 30 euros
An agreeable modern 27-bedroomed hotel with its own restaurant.

MARNE
Châlons-en-Champagne

Hotel d'Angleterre****
Place Mgr. Tissier
Châlons-en-Champagne
Next to Notre-Dame de Vaux
Tel: 00 33 (0)326 68 21 51
Tariff: Double 95-150 euros
An elegant hotel with marble bathrooms, ideal for romantics. Considered the best in town. Lovely Michelin star restaurant.

Le Renard
24 pl de la République
Châlons-en-Champagne
http://le-renard.com/
Tel: 00 33 (0)326 68 03 78
Tariff: Double 71 euros
Guestrooms are a littled dated with gaudy bedspreads and plasticy en-suite facilities. But, they are spacious, in the town centre and have private parking and a good restaurant which serves a stunning gastronomic display. Regional delights include snail brochettes and langoustines and seabass served with pistachio nuts.

Hotels

MARNE
Epernay

Hôtel de la Cloche **
3-5 Place Mendès-France
Epernay
Near to the 19th century church and opposite train station
Tel: 00 33 (0)3 26 55 24 05
Tariff: From 38 euros
There are 19 rooms, 1 with en-suite bathroom, the rest with showers.

Hôtel Berceaux ***
13 rue des Berceaux
Epernay
Near to the 19th century church and opposite train station
Tel: 00 33 (0)3 26 55 28 84
Tariff: From 75 euros
A centrally located hotel. Many of the 29 guestrooms have beamed roofs and ultra-modern en-suite facilities. Seventeen rooms have showers, the rest a bath. All feature television sets and direct dial telephones. The hotel also has its own one Michelin starred restaurant.

Le Royal Champagne
N 2051 Bellvue
F-51160 Champillon Epernay
Located 6km from Epernay and 18km south of Reims
Tel: 00 33 (0)326 52 87
Tariff: Doubles from 300 euros
Closed: January
A luxurious 29-bedroomed hotel in a former coach house built in 1750. It benefits from a luxurious setting above the valley of Epernay on the Mountains of Reims. It affords fantastic views over the river Marne and a patchwork of vines. They say Emperor Napoleon stayed there. Accommodation is in chalets warmly decorated with antique furniture. Its restaurant has been awarded a Michelin star and serves 200 varieties of champagnes. This is the ideal hide-out for champagne lovers who want to visit the vineyards and the great Champagne houses. Free parking.
<u>Getting there:</u> take the A26 towards Reims, exit at junction 25 off the Reims ring road towards Epernay (N51) then towards Champillon taken N 2051.. You'll see a signpost soon after. From Troyes Leave A26 at Châlons, exit St-Gibrien.

Hotels

MARNE
Dizy-Epernay

Prim'Hôtel Bagatelle**
Chemin Les Bas Jardins
Dizy-Epernay
5 mins from Epernay town centre
Tel: 00 33 (0)3 26 51 00 13
Tariff: From 45 euros
Part of the Logis de France chain. Good standard within its range. Reasonable restaurant and mini golf.

MARNE
L'Epine

Aux Armes des Charmpagne****
Place de la Basilique
L'Epine
Located where the A4 and A26 motorways meet opp. the 16th cenury l'Epine Basilica.
Tel: 00 33 (0)3 26 68 03 78
Tariff: From 38 euros
A blend of comfort and tradition featuring a garden, tennis course, mini golf and gastronomic restaurant.

MARNE
Etoges

Château d'Etoges ****
4 Rue Richebourg
Etoges
Tel: 00 33 (0)3 26 59 30 08
Tariff: Doubles 120 euros
Listed as a historical monument this castle was built at the beginning the 17th century by the counts of Anglure. The 20-bedroomed castle was a base for the kings of France while travelling the eastern road between Paris and Strasbourg. It is located in Reims near the vineyards of la "Côte des Blancs". The medieval fortress sits amidst a wooded park with natural fountains. Surrounded by moats and tastefully furnished, the Chateau has been run by the same family for over a century It has a bar and a gastronomic restaurant.
<u>Getting there:</u>
On the A4 motorway exit as Ferté sou Jouarre and follow signs to Chalons. At Chalons cross city centre towards Epernay and then towards Meaux or Montmirail.

Hotels

MARNE
Fèr en Tardenois

Château de Fère
Route De Fismes
Fère En Tardenois
www.ila-chateau.com/fere/
Tel: 00 33 (0)3 23 82 21 13
Tariff: Double 207 euros
Closed: January

The 25 bedroomed chateau is located out of the way on a magnificently picturesque wooded spot 3 miles north of Fère-en-Tardenois. There is a pretty pool overlooking serene fields and the Chateau de Fere ruins next door are very romantic especially when viewed from the rooftop seating area as the sun sets. The gastronomic restaurant offers great wine and food with expert advice on marrying the two.

Getting there: Take A4 direction of Paris, exit at Dormans No. 21, turn right on RD 980 then right again, direction of Fère en Tardenois by D801 & D2. Cross the village of Fère en Tardenois up to the traffic light and turn right direction of Fismes by D967.

MARNE
Reims

**Hôtel Le Crystal **
86 Place Drouet d'Erlon
Reims
Located on a pedestrianised stree off Place Erlon, steps from the Cathedral
Tel: 00 33 (0)326 88 44 44
Tariff: Double 35 euros

The entrance to the hotel is through an easily missed passage and up a flight of stairs. There is a charming birdcage lift and breakfast is in the garden on sunny days.

**Hôtel Bristol **
76 Place Drouet d'Erlon
Reims
Located on a pedestrianised stree off Place Erlon, steps from the Cathedral
Tel: 00 33 (0)326 40 52 25
Tariff: Double 40-50 euros

An old style 40-bedroom attractive hotel with an attractive reception area, clean rooms.with its own supervised parking.

Hotels

Grand Hôtel Continental ***
93 Place Drouet d'Erlo
Reims
www.grandhotelcontinental.com
Located on a pedestrianised stree off Place Erlon, steps from the Cathedral
Tel: 00 33 (0)326 40 39 35
Tariff: Double 40-50 euros
Closed: Christmas
A traditional and elegant 50-roomed hotel. The reception area is grandiose decorated with antiques and pictures.

Grand Hotel Europe ***
29 rue Buirette
Reims
Near Buirette shopping centre
Tel: 00 33 (0)33 26 47 39 39
Tariff: Double 75 euros
A modern hotel with 54 air conditioned rooms, with all mod cons including Wi.Fi.

Hôtel de la Paix ***
9 rue Buirette
Reims
www.bestwestern.com
Near Buirette shopping centre
Tel: 00 33 (0)326 47 75 04
Tariff: Double 80 euros

This 106 bedroomed modern chain hotel is located between the train station and the cathedral. It is unique in that though a modern hotel, it comes with a medieval chapel originally built for Benedictine nuns in the 1200s. The chapel overlooks the garden and the pool. It also has a good restaurant and a bar.

Mercure Reims Cathédrale***
31 Boulevard Paul-Doumer
Reims
www.accor-hotels.com
Located 3 minutes drive from Exit 24 of A24 and minutes from the cathedral.
Tel: 00 33 (0)326 84 49 49
Tariff: Double 106 euros
This air-conditioned chain hotel sits on the banks of the Marne canal, just a 5 minute walk from the town centre and cathedral. Its location close to the autoroute makes it easy to find. Rooms are spacious with mod cons and some overlook the canal.

Hotels

Grand Hôtel des Templiers**
22 rue des Templiers
Reims
Tel: 00 33 (0)326 88 55 08
Tariff: Doubles 200 euros
This old 19th century house, located in a residential road close to the cathedral and city centre and provides luxurious accommodation and great facilities.

Boyer - Les Crayères**
64 Boulevard Henry Vasnier
Reims
www.gerardboyer.com
Tel: 00 33 (0)32682 8080
Tariff: Double 300 euros
Closed: Chrismas &New Year
The castles rooms are extravagantly decorated and is set amidst vineyards and has its own three Michelin starred kitchens. Ideal if what you are looking for is hedonism of the palate, beautiful scenery, seclusion and are prepared for the bill.

MARNE
Sezanne

Croix d'Or**
53 rue de Notre Dame
Sezanne
Tel: 00 33 (0)326 80 61 10
Tariff: from 28 euros
Closed: First 2 weeks Jan
A satisfactory 12 roomed old-style inn. The restaurant is full of antiques.

Relais Champenois**
53 rue de Notre Dame
Sezanne
Tel: 00 33 (0)326 80 61 10
Tariff: from 28 euros
Closed: Feb
A pleasant inn with restaurant.

MARNE
Vertus

Le Thibault IV**
2 Place de la République
Vertus
Tel: 00 33 (0)326 52 01 24
Tariff: Doubles from 54 euros
A comfortable 17 bedroomed Logis de France hotel. It has its own restaurant.

Hotels

AUBE
Bar Sur Aube

Hôtel le Saint Nicolas
2 rue Général de Gaulle
Bar Sur Aube
2 minutes walk from station and town centre
Tel: 00 33 (0)325 27 08 65
Tariff: From 45 euros
Pleasant stone-clad building Several trooms are beamed and feature Provençal blue furniture. Satellite television and telephones are in each room. The place scores highly with tourists because of its outdoor swimming pool and sauna.

AUBE
Essoyes

Hôtel des Canotiers
Locality les Crépadots, Essoyes, Aube en Champage
Take the A5 motorway, exit 22
Tel: 00 33 (0)325 38 61 08
Tariff: From 91 euros
Closed: March
www.hoteldescanotiers.com
This lovely hotel just on the outskirts of the charming village of Essoyes, once the home of Renoir, has a restaurant and guests enjoy the panoramic views over the Champagne vineyards and the River Ource. Free parking.

AUBE
Troyes

Les Comtes de Champagne
56 rue de la Monnaie
Troyes
Tel: 00 33 (0)325 73 11 70
Tariff: From 43 euros
Once the city mint, this timber framed house offers good value accommodation. Many rooms feature the orignal brickwork, fireplaces, beams and elegant double doors. Across the road there are five apartments. Breakfast is served in the glass roofed conservatory and parking is free.

Hôtel Le Royal
22 Boulevard Carnot
Troyes
Tel: 00 33 (0)325 73 19 99
www.royal-hotel-troyes.com
Tariff: Doubles from 70 euros
A reasonable hotel, handy for the train station comes

Hotels

complete with its own restaurant.

Hôtel Le Champ des Oiseaux
20 rue Linard Gonthier
Troyes
Tel: 00 33 (0)325 80 58 50
Tariff: Doubles90 euros
www.champdesoiseaux.com
Idyllically situated in Troyes' oldest quarter right next door the Museum of Modern Art and the Cathedral of Saint Peter and Saint Paul, this 12 bedroomed hotel is decked out with antique furniture and floral prints but has all mod cons. There are two suites and the the Suite Médiévale, is under the oak-beamed eaves. Downstairs is a lovely breakfast room with a stone fireplace but there is no restaurant.

Hôtel La Maison de Rhodes
18 rue Linard Gonthier
Troyes
Tel: 00 33 (0)325 43 11 11
Tariff: Doubles from 94 euros
This is the sister hotel of Hotel Le Champ des Oiseaux and shares its fabulous location. It was once owned by the Templars, this hotel is housed in a typically historic 16th century timbered building with a cobbled courtyard and dainty walkways. Rooms are traditionally rustic and tastefully decorated.

Hôtel de la Poste
35 rue Emile-Zola
Troyes
Tel: 00 33 (0)325 73 05 05
Tariff: Doubles from 100 euros
www.hotel-de-la-poste.com
Both the dining rooms and guestrooms are modern, bright and elegant. There are touches of character around with open beams and exposed brickwork in many places. Luxury is the key watchword however. Private parking.

Le Relais St Jean de la Poste****
51 rue Paillot-de-Montabert
Troyes
Tel: 00 33 (0)325 73 89 90
Tariff: Doubles from 100 euros
A lovely hotel with an historic half timbered facade. 23 air-conditioned rooms are all individually decorated. Intimate bar and impresive buffet breakfast.

Hotels

HAUTE MARNE
Chaumont

Hôtel Les Remparts*
72 rue de Verdun
Chaumont
Located in the town centre near the poster museum
www.hotel-les-remparts.fr
Tel: 00 33 (0)3 25 32 64 40
Tariff: 60-90 euros
This charming hotel, decorated with flower boxes on all three floors of the exterior, offers 18, comfortable, sound-proofed, air-conditioned rooms with satellite TV. There is also a bar and restaurant.

Getting there: From Troyes take the A5 motorway, exit 24 "Chaumont-Semoutiers". From Langres, take the A 31 and A5 motorway.

HAUTE MARNE
Langres

Le Cheval Blanc*
4 rue de L'Estres
Langres
www.hotel-langres.com
Tel: 00 33 (0)3 25 87 07 00
Tariff: 60-90 euros
A quaint 22-room hotel created out of a former historic cistercian abbey - the Church of Saint Amatre - dating back to 834. Many of the features remain and some rooms are still vaulted. All rooms have a TV, telephone and mini bar. It also has its own gastronomic restaurant - Le Diderot. Langres finest option.

Festivals

There's nothing like a festival to make a trip... festive

What: Ramble round the Cadoles
When: 1st May
Where: Les Riceys (Aube)
Tel : 00 33 (0)3 25 29 15 38
www.les-riceys-champagne.com
Every year, a ramble followed by lunch in the country, starts out from Riceys through the vineyards in search of Cadoles.

What: Sedan Medieval festival
When: 21-22nd May
Where: Sedan (Ardennes)
Tel : 00 33 (0)3 25 29 15 38
Medieval festivities take place around the biggest fortress in Europe.Includes jousting, tournaments, markets, medieval street fighting, camps, flag throwing, feasts and the cavalry tournament is a must-see, for the medieval combat. Kick off at 7pm

What: Joan of Arc Festival (Fêtes Johanniques)
When: June
Where: Reims (Marne)
Tel :00 33 (0) 3 26 77 45 00
www.reims-tourisme.com
An annual festival celebrating the memory of French patron saint Joan of Arc with a succession of shows and historical living epics. In an atmosphere of the Middle Ages, visitors can stroll through the stalls of a medieval market, watch a grand spectacle of music and light, and admire the Grand Procession of the Kings of France crowned at Reims (a cast of 2,000 in period costume accompany Joan of Arc and Charles VII).

What: The Fête du Pétard
When: June
Where: Langres (Haute Marne)
Compagnie des Hallebardiers de Langres
Tel : 00 33 (0)3 25 90 77 40
A traditional festival relating to a famous episode in the Wars of Religion. One night in 1591, members of the League from Lorraine tried to take the city by surprise by setting a mine, or "pétard" (a bowl filled with black powder) against the door of the Hotel de Ville. The watchful Halberdiers, thwarted the effort. The Pétard became a trophy and an official festival to celebrate the event was perpetuated. A great, entertaining, procession winds its way through the town and round

Festivals

the ramparts of Langres, with entertainments along its route. All night long the town will be alive with plays, music, the plastic arts, and festivities.

What: Festival Furies
When: June
Where: Chàlons-en-Champagne (Marne)
Tel : 00 33 (0)3 26 65 90 06
www.festivals-furies.com
The annual Furies Festival is a circus and street theatre event that takes place throughout the town of Châlons-en-Champagne. Companies come from all over the world to showcase their improvisation and creativity.

What: The Aymon Folk Festival
When: 1st Sat in August
Where: Bogny-sur-Meuse (Ardennes)
Features music performed by both local and national bands in an idyllic setting under the stars in the main square of of Bogny-sur-Meuse. Refer to page 24 for more information.

What: Champagne Route Festival
When: August
Where: Aube
Association pour la Promotion du Vignoble Champenois
Tel : 00 33 (0)3 25 43 72 72
www.vignoble-champagne.com
Wine-growers open their cellars to the public for a whole weekend. With your "champagne glass pass", you enjoy champagne tastings at the various hospitality points. Villages provide the entertainments - exhibitions of paintings, photographs, and crafts.

What: The Foire de Châlons
When: August - September
Where: Châlons-en-Champagne (Marne)
Tel: 00 33 (0)3 26 21 85 80
A huge exhibition of everything related to the Champagne-Ardenne region, held in Châlons' exhibition centre. Includes cows, agricultural materials and local produce to cars, arts and crafts, health, interior design and tourism. The programme attracts more than 250,000 visitors every year.

What: Puppet Festival
When: Charleville Mézières (Ardennes)
Where: 15 Oct to 24 Oct
Tel : 00 33 (0)3 24 59 94 94
www.marionnette.com
The most important puppet festival in the world. Refer to page 31 for more information.

Practicalities - Driving in France

Driving along the well-maintained roads and motorways in France is a pleasure. But be sure not to break the law.

En Route Essentials:
To comply with French motoring regulations, please note what is and is not essential:

It is essential:
- To have a full UK driving licence and all motoring documents.
- To be over the age of 18 - even if you have passed your test in the UK.
- Not to exceed 90km/h in the first year after passing your test.
- To display a GB sticker or Euro number plate.
- To carry a red warning triangle.
- To wear rear and front seat belts.
- To affix headlamp diverters. These are widely available in motoring shops or DIY with black masking tape.

It is not essential:
- To have a green card although very helpful.
- To have yellow headlights.

Traffic News:
Tune in to Autoroute FM107.7 for French traffic news in English and French.

Speed Limits:
In France speed limits are shown in kilometres per hour **not** miles per hour. Always adhere to these speed limits as in France they are strictly enforced and punishable with a fine or even a ban:

	MPH	km/h
Toll motorways	81	130
Dual Carriageways	68	110
Other Roads	56	90
Towns	30	50

When raining, these speed limits are reduced by 6mph on the roads and 12mph on the motorway. In fog, speed is restricted to 31mph. As well as speed traps, it is useful to know that entrance and exit times through the toll booths can be checked on your toll ticket and may be used as evidence of speeding!

Practicalities - Driving in France

Motorways & Roads:
French motorways (autoroutes) are marked by blue and white A signs. Many motorways are privately owned and outside towns a toll charge (péage) is usually payable and can be expensive. This can be paid by credit card (Visa Card, Eurocard, Mastercard), or euros at automatic gates, so be prepared.

Contact a tourist board for the exact cost. if you have access to the internet click on
www.autoroutes.fr.

Roads are indicated as:

A roads -
Autoroutes - Motorways where a toll is probably payable.

N Roads -
routes nationales - toll free, single lane roads. Slower than A roads.

D roads -
Routes départementales - scenic alternatives to A roads.

C roads -
routes communales - country roads.

Breakdown on Motorways:
If you should break down on the motorway and you do not have breakdown cover, **DON'T PANIC**, you can still get assistance.

There are emergency telephones stationed every mile and a half on the motorway. These are directly linked to the local police station. The police are able to locate you automatically and arrange for an approved repair service to come to your aid.

Naturally there is a cost for this and fees are regulated. Expect to pay around £50 for labour plus parts and around £55 for towing.

An extra 25% supplement is also charged if you break down between 6pm and 8am and any time on Saturdays, Sundays and national holidays.

At the garage, ensure you ask for un Ordre de Réparation (repair quote) which you should sign. This specifies the exact nature of the repairs, how long it will take to repair your vehicle and, importantly, the cost!

Practicalities - Driving in France

Roadside Messages:
For safety's sake, it is very important to be aware of the roadside messages:

Carrefour	Crossroad
Déviation	Diversion
Priorité à droite	Give way to traffic on the right
Péage	Toll
Ralentir	Slow down
Vous n'avez pas la priorité	Give way
Rappel	Restriction continues
Sens unique	One way
Serrez à droite/ à gauche	Keep right/ Keep left
Véhicules lents	Slow vehicles
Gravillons	Loose chippings
Chaussée Déformée	Uneven road and temporary surface
Nids de Poules	Potholes

Drink Driving:
French law dictates that a 50g limit of alcohol is allowed - just one glass of wine. Exceed this limit and you risk confiscation of your license, impounding of the car, a prison sentence or an on-the-spot fine between £20 to £3,000!

Tyre Pressure:
It is crucial to ensure that your tyres are at the correct pressure to cater for heavy loads. Make sure you do not exceed the car's maximum carrying weight. The following table gives a guide to typical loads:

		Weight	
1 case of	Qty	kg	lbs
Wine	x 2	15kg	33lbs
Champagne	x12	22kg	48lbs
Beer 25cl	x 2	8kg	18lbs

Filling Up:
To fill up, head for petrol stations attached to the hypermarkets as these offer the best value fuel. Petrol stations on the motorway - autoroutes - tend to be more expensive. Though sterling and travellers cheques are not accepted, credit cards usually are. Some petrol stations have automated payment facilities by credit card. These are generally 24 hour petrol stations and tend to be unmanned in the evening but do not rely on them for fuel salvation as they often do not accept international credit cards!

Petrol grades are as follows:

Unleaded petrol -
l'essence sans plomb.

Practicalities - Driving in France

Available in 95 & 98 grades - equates to UK premium and super grades respectively.

Leaded petrol -
l'essence or Super
Graded as:
90 octane (2 star),
93 octane (3 star)
97 octane (4 star).
Gazole - Diesel Fuel
GPL - LPG (liquefied petroleum gas)

IMPORTANT!

- IN **TOWNS** IF THERE ARE NO STOP SIGNS AT THE INTERSECTION, CARS MUST YIELD TO THE RIGHT

- ON A **MAIN ROAD** CARS HAVE PRIORITY OVER TRAFFIC JOINING FROM A SIDE-ROAD ON THE RIGHT.

- CHILDREN UNDER 10 ARE NOT ALLOWED TO TRAVEL IN THE FRONT

- DRIVE ON THE RIGHT, OVERTAKE ON THE LEFT

Emergency Phrases:

Please, help
Aidez-moi s'il vous plaît

My car has broken down
Ma voiture est en panne

I have run out of petrol
Je suis en panne d'essence

The engine is overheating
Le moteur surchauffe

There is a problem with the brakes
Il y a un problème de freins

I have a flat tyre
J'ai un pneu crevé

The battery is flat
La batterie est vide

There is a leak in the petrol tank/in the radiator
Il y a une fuite dans le réservoir d'essence/dans le radiateur

Can you send a mechanic/breakdown van?
Pouvez-vous envoyer un mécanicien/une dépanneuse?

Can you tow me to a garage?
Pouvez-vous me remorquer jusqu'à un garage?

I have had an accident
J'ai eu un accident

The windscreen is shattered
Le pare-brise est cassé

Call an ambulance
Appelez une ambulance

Practicalities - Driving in France

Accidents:
If you do have an accident you must fill out a damage assessment form. Get this from your insurance company before you leave. It must be signed by the other party and in the event of a dispute or a refusal to complete the form you should immediately obtain a constat d'huissier. This is a written report from a bailiff (huisser). In the event of a dispute call the police so that you can make out an official report. If someone is injured call the SAMU (15) or the fire brigade (18). The police are only called out to accidents when someone is injured or a driver is under the influence of alcohol or the accident impedes the flow of traffic.

Parking:
Illegal parking in France can be penalised by a fine, wheel clamping or vehicle removal. Park wherever you see a white dotted line or if there are no markings at all.

There are also numerous pay and display meters. (horodateurs) where small change is required to buy a ticket. The ticket should be displayed inside the car windscreen on the driver's side.

If you find a blue parking zone (zone bleue), this will be indicated by a blue line on the pavement or road and a blue signpost with a white letter P. If there is a square under the P then you have to display a cardboard disc which has various times on it. They allow up to two and a half hours parking time. The discs are available in supermarkets or petrol stations and are sometimes given away free. Ask for a **disque de stationnement.**

Services:
On the motorways every

10km	rest areas for short stops
40km	service stations and restaurants
100+km	motels for overnight stops

By the way, the beginning of a town is marked by the town name - a bar through the town name marks the end of the town.

Practicalities - Money Matters

Currency:
The currency used in France is the Euro. This is made up of notes and Euro coins and cents. When you are looking at a price tag, menu or receive a receipt be aware that unlike the British system of separating pounds and pence with a decimal point, in France there is no decimal point, Euros and cents are separated by a comma.

Unlimited currency may be taken into France but you must declare bank notes of 50,000 Euros or more if you are bringing this back.

Currency Exchange:
Changing money from sterling to Euros can be expensive. Use your credit card to pay for goods abroad, as credit card companies tend to give a better rate of exchange. If you require cash. change your money in the UK where it can be a little more competitive than in France.

In France you can also change money and cash travellers cheques at the post office (PTT), banks, stations and private bureaux de change.

You can also make a purchase in the hypermarkets in Calais in sterling, as change is given in Euros without commission. Though convenient, always be aware of the exchange rate. Some shops do take advantage.

Travellers cheques can be used as cash. At a French bank you will receive the face value - no commission.

Most banks in France do not accept Eurocheques

Credit Cards:
Credit cards are widely accepted To use your credit card ensure that you have your passport handy as you may be expected to produce it.

If your card has been rejected in a shop or restaurant, it could be that their card reading machine does not recognise it - some French credit cards have a 'puce', a microchip with security information on it. In Britain this system is becoming widespread. However if your credit card company has not yet supplied you with a Chip and Pin French tourist authorities recommend you say:

Practicalities - Money Matters

Les cartes anglaises ne sont pas des cartes à puce, mais à band magnétique. Ma carte est valable et je vous serais reconnaissant d'en demander la confirmation auprès de votre banque ou de votre centre de traitement.'

which means:
English cards don't have an information chip, but a magnetic band. My card is valid and I would be grateful if you would confirm this with your bank or processing centre.'

If you need to contact:

Barclaycard
Tel: +44 (0)1604 234234

Visa
Tel: +44 (0)1383 621166

Visa in France
Tel: 01 45 67 84 84
Cashpoints:
You can use your cashpoint card to get local currency from cash-dispensing machines. This service is available at major banks such as: Crédit Lyonnais, Crédit Agricole and Crédit Mutuel. If the machine bears the same logo as that displayed on your card, such as Visa or Delta, then you can insert your card and follow the instructions. These are likely to be in English as your card will be recognised as British.

Punch in your PIN and press the button marked **Envoi.** When prompted tell the machine how much you want in French francs. You will see phrases such as:

Tapez votre code secret - Enter your pin

Veuillez patienter -
Please wait

Opération en cours -
Money on its way!

Shopping:
Shops opening hours are below though supermarkets and garages tend to stay open all day:

Open	9.00 am
Close lunch-time	12.00 noon
Open again	2.00 pm
Close finally	5.00-7.00 pm

Most shops are closed on Sunday and some on Monday. Supermarket trolleys (les chariots) require a (refundable) 1 euro piece.

179

Practicalities - Out and About in France

Taxi!
It is cheaper to hail a taxi in the street or cab ranks indicated by the letter 'T' than order one by telephone. This is because a telephone- requested taxi will charge for the time taken to reach you. Taxi charges are regulated. The meter must show the minimum rate on departure and the total amount (tax included) on arrival. If the driver agrees that you share the taxi, he has the right to turn the meter back to zero at each stop showing the minimum charge again.

Tipping:
Tipping is widely accepted in France. However, restaurant menus with the words 'servis compris' indicate that service is included but small change can be left. The following is the accepted norm for tipping:

Restaurants service usually included	Optional
Cafés service usually included	Optional
Hotels	No
Hairdressers	2 euros
Taxis	10%
Porters	2 euros
Cloakroom attendants	Small change
Toilets	Small change

Public Holidays:
Most French shops, business and and even restaurants will be shut on the following days. Check in advance if you require a restaurant booking on any of these days:

Jan 1	New Year	Jour de l'an
Apr*	Easter Monday	Lundi de Pâques
May 1	Labour Day	Fête du Travail
May 8	Victory Day	Armistice1945
May*	Ascension	Ascension
May*	Whitsun	Lundi de Pentecôte
July 14	Bastille Day	Fête nationale
Aug 15	Assumption	Assomption
Nov 1	All Saints'	Toussaint
Nov 11	Armistice Day	Armistice 1918
Dec 25	Christmas	Noël

*Dates change each year.

School Holidays:

Summer Holidays	30 Jun-6 Sept
Autumn Half Term	27 Oct-5Nov
Christmas Holidays	22 Dec-7 Jan
Winter Half Term	2 Feb-18 Feb
Easter Holidays	30 Mar-15 Apr

These are approximate dates and do change a little every year

No Smoking!
It is forbidden to smoke in public places. However, there are quite often spaces reserved in cafés and restaurants for smokers.

Practicalities - Out and About in France

Caught on the Hop!
Cafés allow you to use their toilets for free. Shopping centres also have facilities. If you see a white saucer, place a coin or two in it. In the streets you may see the Sanisette, a white cylindrical building. Insert the required coin in the slot to open the door. After use the Sanisette cleans itself.

Pharmacy:
These are recognised by their green cross sign. Staff tend to be highly qualified so are able to give medical advice on minor ailments, provide first aid and prescribe some drugs. Some drugs are only available via a doctor's prescription (ordonnance).

Medical Aid:
As members of the EU, the British can get urgent medical treatment in France at reduced costs on production of a form E111 available from the Department of Health and Social Security. A refund can then be obtained in person or by post from the local Social Security Offices (Caisse Primaire d'Assurance Maladie).

Doctor:
Any pharmacy will have an address of a doctor. Consultation fees are generally about £15.00. Make sure you have your E111 form which means you can claim the fees back. Ask for a Feuille de Soins (Statement of Treatment) if you are insured.

Electricity:
You will need a continental adapter plug (with round pins). The voltage in France is 220V and 240V in the UK.

Television/Video Tapes:
French standard TV broadcast system is SECAM whereas in the UK it is PAL. Ordinary video cassettes bought in France will show only in black and white. French video tapes cannot be played on British videos. Ask for VHS PAL system.

Emergency Numbers:

Police	17
Fire	18
Ambulance	15
Operator	13
Directory enquiries	12

Practicalities - Out and About in France

Phoning Home:
French telephone numbers have 10 digits. To call UK dial the international code 00 44 then the UK number minus the first 0. To call France from the UK dial the international code 00 33 then the French number minus the first 0. Phonecards (Télécartes) are widely used and available at travel centres, post offices, tobacconists (tabacs), newsagents and shops displaying the Télécarte sign. You will need one to use a telephone box. 50 units costs 7.41 euros. 120 units costs 14.88 euros. Instructions in English are generally included. Between 8am and 7pm a phone call from France to the UK costs 0.25 euros per minute and 0.15 euros at weekends starting 2pm on Satudays.

Cheap rate (50% extra time) is between 22.30hrs-08.00hrs Monday to Friday, 14.00hrs-08.00hrs Saturday, all day Sunday & public holidays. To call the UK dial 00, at the dialling tone dial 44 followed by the phone number and omit 0 from the STD code. To call:
The operator dial :   13
Directory Enquiries dial :   12

Writing Home:
Post offices (PTT) are open Monday to Friday during office hours and half day on Saturday. Smaller branches close between noon and 2pm. Stamps can also be bought from tobacconists.

What's the Time?
French summer starts on the last Sunday in March at 2am and ends on the last Sunday in October at 3am. Time is based on Central European Time (Greenwich Mean Time + 1 hour in winter and + 2 hours in summer). The clocks are put forward 1 hour in the spring and put back 1 hour in the autumn.

Passports:
You need a full 10- year EU passport. Non-EU nationals require a visa and regulations vary according to nationality.

Pet Passports:
Since 28th February 2000, cats and dogs can travel abroad without being subjected to six months quarantine. A blood test is required and a microchip is fitted. Not more than 48 hours before return, the animal must be treated for tics and tapeworms. PETS helpline 0870 2411 710.

Practicalities - Conversion Tables

What's Your Size?
When buying clothes in France, check the conversion tables below to find out your size

Women's Shoes

GB	FR	GB	FR
3 =	35$^{1}/_{2}$	5$^{1}/_{2}$ =	39
3$^{1}/_{2}$ =	36	6 =	39$^{1}/_{2}$
4 =	37	6$^{1}/_{2}$ =	40
4$^{1}/_{2}$ =	37$^{1}/_{2}$	7 =	40$^{1}/_{2}$
5 =	38	8 =	41$^{1}/_{2}$

Women's Dresses/Suits

GB	FR	GB	FR
8 =	36	14 =	42
10 =	38	16 =	44
12 =	40	18 =	46

Women's Blouses/Sweaters

GB	FR	GB	FR
30 =	36	36 =	42
32 =	38	38 =	44
34 =	40	40 =	46

Men's Shirts

GB	FR	GB	FR
14$^{1}/_{2}$ =	37	16 =	41
15 =	38	16$^{1}/_{2}$ =	42
15$^{1}/_{2}$ =	39/40	17 =	43

Men's Suits

GB	FR	GB	FR
36 =	46	42 =	52
38 =	48	44 =	54
40 =	50	46 =	56

Men's Shoes

GB	FR	GB	FR
7 =	40	10 =	43
8 =	41	11 =	44
9 =	42	12 =	45
		13 =	46

Weights and Measures:

Distance 1.6 km = 1 mile
Weight 1 kg = 2.20lbs
Liquid 4.54 litres = 1 gallon
Liquid 1 litre = 1.76 pints
Length 1m = 39.37inches
Area 1sq metre = 1.196 sq yds

Speed

kpm	mph	kpm	mph
50	31	100	62
70	43	110	68
80	50	120	75
90	56	130	81

Practicalities - Custom Guidelines

**In theory there are no limits on the amount of alcohol or tobacco for personal use.
In practice exceeding the Advisory Guidelines, means you could be stopped**

Since 1st January 1993, you are permitted to bring back as much alcohol and tobacco as you like, but it must be for personal use only. So you can happily stock up for Christmas or parties or weddings.

Although H. M. Customs and Excise have no authority to limit the amount you bring back into this country they do have the right to stop you if your purchases exceed the Advisory Guidelines. In this case you may be required to prove that the goods are for your own personal use. That means you cannot buy goods on behalf of anyone else, even your own mother!

If you are stopped, remember that the H.M. Customs officer is looking for bootleggers or those intent on resale. Other products such as mineral water, or any other non-alcoholic or food products, are not limited in any way.

Enjoy.

Advisory Guidelines
as set by H.M. Customs & Excise

Wine	90 litres
Spirits	10 litres
Fortified wine	20 litres
Beer	110 litres
Cigarettes	3200
Cigars	200
Cigarillos	400
Tobacco	3 kilogram

Note: People under 17 are not allowed to bring in tobacco and alcohol